Lonely, but Not Alone

A Journey Out of Brokenness

PEGGY SKAGGS VESSER

WESTBOW
P R E S S®
A DIVISION OF THOMAS NELSON
& ZONDERVAN

THE HOLY BIBLE, NEW INTERNATIONAL VERSION®, NIV® Copyright © 1973, 1978, 1984, 2011 by Biblica, Inc.® Used by permission. All rights reserved worldwide.

Scripture taken from the NEW AMERICAN STANDARD BIBLE®, Copyright © 1960, 1962, 1963, 1968, 1971, 1972, 1973, 1975, 1977, 1995 by The Lockman Foundation. Used by permission."

Scripture taken from the King James Version of the Bible.

WestBow Press books may be ordered through booksellers or by contacting:

WestBow Press
A Division of Thomas Nelson & Zondervan
1663 Liberty Drive
Bloomington, IN 47403
www.westbowpress.com
1 (866) 928-1240

ISBN: 978-1-9736-1173-8 (sc)
ISBN: 978-1-9736-1172-1 (e)

Print information available on the last page.

WestBow Press rev. date: 1/4/2018

. . . I have summoned you by name,
you are Mine.

When you pass through the waters,
I will be with you;
and when you pass through the rivers,
they will not sweep over you.

When you walk through the fire,
you will not be burned; . . .

For I am the Lord your God,
The Holy one of Israel, your savior; . . .
and because I love you.

Do not be afraid;
for I am with you; . . .

Isaiah 43: 1 − 5 (NIV)

DEDICATION TO YOU
May the words I've shared in this book,
reveal more of God's holy Love for you,
quickly usher His comfort and His strength to you,
and give you <u>His</u> peace that passes all understanding.

Forewords

Peggy Vesser's journey is the story of victory in the face of heartache and heartbreak. Her story will help you find the strength and victory that only Christ can give in the face of the storm.

Dr. H. Dean Haun
Senior Pastor | FIRST BAPTIST CHURCH, MORRISTOWN, TN

Peggy's story demonstrates how a woman of God is able to rise above the deep sorrow that comes through the death of a spouse; . . . not just once, but twice. Her love and losses, along with seasons of grieving and acceptance, have strengthened her quiet spirit and formed her beautiful character. Peggy invites the reader to journey into her private world as she discloses the agonizing and tender moments of saying 'goodbye' to the precious loves of her life. Her testimony is an example of healthy and Godly grieving as she draws from the strength of family, friends, and her Lord, Jesus Christ. Peggy offers hope and encouragement to others who grieve as she reminds them that God has a plan and a purpose for their lives beyond their darkest moments.

Beth Greene
LPC AND FRIEND

Acknowledgments

My special thanks goes to my three children; Mark, Pam, and Steven, and their families, for their love and support.

To my friend, Beth Greene, who believed in me and pushed me to get this book done.

To my pastor, Dr. Dean Haun, who was so helpful and encouraging when this project first began.

To my editor, Rebecca Bradley, of American Copy Editors, for her knowledge and skill.

And last, but certainly not the least, to my Lord and Savior, Jesus Christ, without whose great Love and the mending of my broken spirit, this book would not have been written.

Contents

Part III: The Days That Followed

Prologue

There are probably very few of you who have not experienced some type of brokenness. If you are not experiencing it now, you already have, or you will in the future. Being in the place of brokenness of spirit is not a place any of us would choose to be; but sometimes God allows us to be there, perhaps to teach us, to get our attention focused back on Him, or so He can reaffirm His love for us and His presence in our lives.

Brokenness can come in many forms — grief over the loss of a loved one, financial loss, loss of health, marriages ending in divorce, etc. I'm going to share with you my personal experience of brokenness, a kind of unyielding brokenness, that left me feeling that my life was literally in pieces, and that I was no longer a whole or complete person.

My story; however, is not just about brokenness, although it is through this experience that I have come to where I am today. Rather, my story is about God's grace. When the children of Israel were wandering in the wilderness, God provided them daily manna to eat. He also told them to gather only what they would need for each day. I believe that is the way He gives us His grace when difficulties come our way — in just the right amount we need to sustain us each day.

There is a song I once heard, entitled *Only By Grace*. It basically says that it is not by our endeavors, but only by His grace are we able to stand. So, my story is written, not to boast, and tell you what Peggy Skaggs Vesser can do, but more to say that God is able, and when I can't, HE CAN!

My story begins when a major storm came into my life in August, 1994. It was written from notes I kept in a journal. It is prefaced with information about my family and our lives.

My prayer, in sharing my story, or rather, the revelation of God's grace in my life, is that it will help someone reading this who may be struggling through that 'valley of the shadow of death,' or perhaps it may help someone who unknowingly is getting ready to enter that valley, or whatever your life's struggle may be.

Charles and Peggy Skaggs
October 12, 1965

Part One
Charles Skaggs

Charles and I met in high school, when I was a 15 year-old freshman. He said he spotted me across the room in the choir, and determined then, he was going to take me out. After much begging and pleading, my mother finally allowed me to have a date with him. Our first date was to attend the Sweetheart Banquet at First Baptist Church.

We dated all through high school. He left in early February of 1964 to go into the Navy. He returned from basic training in late May and we became engaged before he left to go back to begin his three-year term in service to our country.

My parents were not surprised, but they did want us to wait until Charles was discharged from service before we got married. We had planned to wait, but three years seemed such a long time when you are young and in love. We married October 12, 1965, when he was home on leave. We planned our wedding in four days and were married in the chapel of our church, with just family and a few friends. Afterwards, we left for a short honeymoon in Gatlinburg, Tennessee.

For financial reasons, we decided I would remain at home with my parents and keep my job. Upon returning to Maryland, Charles was transferred to Norfolk, Virginia, where he remained until his discharge in February of 1967.

Each weekend, he and a friend would make the long drive home so we could be together. Each Sunday afternoon, we would say our 'teary' goodbyes. I would usually spend the rest of the day in our room, crying and listening to Andy Williams or Johnny Mathis love songs. The rest of my week would be spent with work and the anticipation of Friday night, when he would be home again. When his discharge came, we moved into a two-bedroom duplex and began our life together as a real married couple!

I continued working until the birth of our first child, Mark, who was born in March, 1969. By that time, we had purchased a small house. Charles was working as a supervisor for a local construction company, and I was loving being a stay-at-home mom. Our daughter, Pam, was born two years later in October, 1971. The only thing to mar our happiness was the death of Charles' mother, earlier that year. But, God is good — He took one from us and gave us another to love.

Our lives were simple but fulfilling. Charles was a good husband. He was a quiet man who was steady and dependable, one in whom I had complete trust, and one on whom I depended a great deal. I knew he would gladly have given his life for me or our children. He worked hard all his life, sometimes in jobs he disliked, to provide for his family. We did not have a lot of material possessions, but we did have mutual love and respect for one another.

He was also a very good father. He was strict with the children in the things that mattered, but not one of them ever had a reason to doubt his love for them, because he spent time with them, and showed his love in many different ways.

Charles was well-known and respected for his service in our church. He was very involved in its television ministry. It began with a radio ministry when he was in high school. He would go to the local radio station each Sunday and borrow the necessary equipment to broadcast the evening worship service. When the service was over, he would return the equipment. After his discharge from the Navy, he resumed this role.

It was Charles who inspired and encouraged our pastor and church leaders to start a television ministry. It began with a one-camera system. At that time, technology was not as advanced as it is now. Every Sunday morning, Charles would go down past the First Methodist Church, climb a telephone pole (in his Sunday suit, I might add!), and make the necessary connections to get our service on the air, over cable television. He had a deep desire to send out the gospel message to those in our community who would never have come to the church building. He continued working in this ministry throughout his life. Charles was the youngest deacon to be ordained in our church at that time, at age 27. He later served as Chairman of Deacons, and was on many committees throughout the years. When our new sanctuary was built, he was involved in the design of the new studios. He used a week of his vacation to move the sound system and equipment from the old sanctuary to the new worship center.

I too, was involved in many of our church ministries, mainly through the music ministry and children's programs. Our children often said we were at the church every time the doors were opened. This was probably true. They were also involved in Sunday School, choirs, Royal Ambassadors (RAs), and Girls in Action (GA). As teenagers, they participated in youth ministry activities. We went on many youth mission trips, Charles as a bus driver and chaperone, and I, as a cook, backyard Bible teacher, and chaperone.

Most of our social life revolved around family and church activities. We spent many times with our good friends, Dale and Eleanor Rose. Many nights and weekends were spent with them and their girls, either at their home or ours. There were many opportunities to develop our closeness and friendship as couples. We also met once a month with four couples for dinner and fellowship.

As our children got older, their activities with school and sports kept us very busy. Both Mark and Pam accepted Christ at an early age; Mark at age seven, in our pastor's office, and Pam, at age seven, at home in her room one night when she and I were alone together. Steven was eight when he made his decision.

When Pam was five, I went to work as a preschool teacher in a local preschool program. It was a good job, and since it was part-time, I was able to be at home in the afternoons, and also be involved in some of the children's school activities. This was also the year that Charles' dad became ill and came to live with us for a brief time. Eventually, he went into a nursing home, and died six weeks later. The storms had begun!

In November, 1969, our third child, Steven, was born. Mark and Pam were eleven and eight respectively, and it was almost like starting all over again! But, we were so thankful to have him, and later on, after losing Charles, I was especially thankful.

In the beginning of my seventh month, I began having problems with the pregnancy. I was put to bed to wait out the rest of the time until his birth. There was a real concern for his health, and mine as well, had I gone into labor too soon. Many of my church friends came to our home every day (organized by my friend Donna Lovelace), and stayed with me until Charles would get home from work. They either cooked while there, or brought food that was already prepared, and took care of anything that needed to be to be done in our home. This went on for four weeks. They performed such a wonderful ministry to our family during that time and we were so grateful.

When I was five weeks from delivery, I began having problems again. It was decided that I needed a C-section. After his birth, one of Steven's lungs collapsed, causing even more problems. Yet another storm! He was kept in the Neonatal Intensive Care Unit (NICU) at the University of Tennessee hospital for 10 days and released to come home. God is so good — he was not left with any permanent damage.

Our lives settled into a normal routine (if you could call it normal with two school-aged children and a newborn!). Each morning, I took Mark to middle school, Pam to elementary school, Steven to my parents, and then went on to my job at the Preschool center. My dad was retired and he and my mom kept Steven for me.

Charles & Peggy Skagg's Children
Mark, Pam, and Steven

In 1982, a dream of mine was realized. Our Child Care Committee asked me to begin a weekday preschool program in our own church, which I did. I retired in May of 2015, after working for 33 years in this ministry.

In March of 1989, my father passed away. The beautiful part was that he became a Christian at the ripe old age of 75! It occurred in his hospital room. God, in His grace, allowed me the opportunity to be present when it happened. So, even in this very real storm, our family still had reason for praise and rejoicing. Nevertheless, losing my daddy was very difficult. He was the first one on my side of the family to pass away. He was the one to whom we all turned for wisdom and advice. It was a huge loss to our family.

In February of 1994, Charles took the early retirement option from his company and went to work at our church as the Director of Properties. It was such a natural progression for him. He had worked there since his early 20s in a volunteer capacity. But, it was not to be for long.

In August of that same year, a storm of such intensity came into my life, that it literally turned my world, that I thought was so safe and secure, upside down. It came suddenly, and without warning, and swiftly brought me to my knees, where I was to be found for many months ahead!

The next several pages are taken from a journal that I kept. If you have a need for comfort or hope, I pray these words will strengthen you.

MONDAY, AUGUST 8, 1994

"Bad things do happen to good people — our response to those things is what is important."

~Bless Your Heart, Series II,
Heartland Samplers, Inc.

"Know therefore, that the Lord your God, is God; He is the faithful God, keeping His covenant of love to a thousand generations of those who love Him and keep His commands."
Deuteronomy 7:9 (NIV)

It was Monday morning. It started out like so many Monday mornings in our nearly 29 years of marriage. Little did I know that the events of this particular morning would change my life forever!

Charles moved quietly around our bedroom getting ready to go to work. I was on summer break from my job as the weekday preschool director at our church and was staying in bed for a few more minutes. He thought I was asleep and was trying not to awaken me. He did not say goodbye, he just went into the kitchen, got his juice, and left for work.

Charles also worked at our church. He had started in late March as the Director of Properties and Maintenance. I knew he had a really busy schedule for the week. In fact, he had asked our 14-year-old son, Steven, to come to the church later with me to assist him.

Steven and I arrived around 9:00 a.m. He went on to find his dad and I went into my office to begin preparation for opening up the preschool again from the summer break. Sometime around 10:00 a.m., Charles stuck his head in the door to say, "Hello." I asked him, "Hi, Honey, what are you doing today?" He rolled his eyes, gave a sigh, and said, "What am I not doing today, would be a better question!"

I do not remember what comment, if any, that I made to him. I do remember; however, thinking how tired he looked. In fact, he had been looking that way for a couple of weeks, so much so, that I had questioned him at length about it over the weekend. On the previous Friday evening, we had discussed how stressed he had been feeling. How I wish I had

8

said something encouraging, or just gotten up from my desk and given him a hug! My mind; however, was already geared to my job and its responsibilities.

I worked on, in the preschool room, which was adjacent to my office, for most of the morning. Sometime before noon, I was back in my office again, working at my desk. Through my open door, I could see Charles, standing in the doorway of the Fellowship Hall, talking with someone. Steven appeared in my door at that time wanting change to get a soft drink. A few minutes later, Charles came into my office and just sat down on the floor. He looked very strange, so I asked him what was wrong. He complained of nausea and dizziness. He also said, "My throat is absolutely killing me!" I asked if his throat were sore. He said it was not, nor had it been sore; it had just come on suddenly. Then, he asked me to get us some lunch. He was extremely agitated and irritable, not like himself at all.

Steven left to go get his dad a Sprite and I began reaching down to get my purse out of the drawer to get them some lunch. When I raised up, Charles was now lying on the floor. At that time, someone knocked on my door. As I went to see who it was, Charles got up and went into the adjoining school room. I was detained only two or three minutes and then went into the room.

Charles was sitting on a chair and was looking really bad. Steven returned with the Sprite. Charles took a couple of sips. I went over to the sink to get a wet paper towel for his forehead. I heard him begin to moan. I looked around. He was beginning to sway as though he were going to faint. I said to Steven, "Quick, Steven, let's get him on the floor before he passes out!" We eased him down on the floor, and I put the paper towel on his head.

Up to this point, I thought he might have some kind of virus. However, he began flexing his fingers and speaking of pain and tingling in both his arms. His facial color was not good either. According to Steven, Charles had earlier lifted a utility trailer and hooked it to a van. He said after he finished, his dad's face was beaded in perspiration, his speech was hurried, and he just did not look well at all.

My heart raced as I called upstairs to the office to locate Jim, the business administrator. Helen, the receptionist, said he had already left for lunch. When I explained what was happening, she said she would call him. I had just hung up the phone and walked back over to Charles, when our friend, Clay Krummel, came running into the room. Behind him were a couple of secretaries and several maintenance people. Clay felt Charles' arms, which by this time, were cold and clammy. Clay said we needed to call 911. I nodded in agreement. One of the secretaries went into my office and made the call. One of the maintenance people went outside and stationed herself by the door to wait to direct the EMS crew to the room where Charles lay.

I knew, the one thing I had feared so long, was finally happening. Charles was in the early stages of a heart attack. He also realized what was happening. As I knelt on the floor beside him, and everyone else stood around us, he began to cry, and to say over and over, "I'm so sorry, I'm so sorry."

Only Steven and I knew the significance of his words. Clay kept telling him there was nothing for which to apologize. But I knew, and so did Steven, the apology was meant for his family, for the trouble he felt he was causing us.

On Thursday night of the past week, we had been sitting on our front porch, in the late evening, as we often did, to talk and have a few moments alone together at the end of the day. We were discussing our friend and neighbor, Duane Kelly, who, we had just learned, had a mild heart attack that day while on a business trip to Florida. I made the statement to Charles, "Honey, that could just as easily have been you." He did not say a word. I had tried for years to get him to stop smoking. What prophetic words to come out of my mouth! But standing there in that room with Steven, watching the EMS people as they brought in the gurney to take him to the hospital, I could have cut my tongue out for having made such a statement!

Someone eased Steven out of the room. He was quite visibly upset. Another of the secretaries came and stood with her arm around me. I cried briefly, but then a strange calmness came over me — or perhaps, it was numbness. I do not remember praying a specific prayer other than thinking, "Lord, help us!" I am sure; however, that everyone in that room was praying. And later on, I learned that all the children were outside getting ready to go to summer church camp. Someone told them what had happened, and they all stopped and prayed for Charles and our family. That day, I began to understand the real power of prayer.

I gathered up my things, got Steven, and left to go to the hospital. Someone offered to drive us, but somehow, I knew I would be needing the car for a trip to Knoxville, where there was more advanced care available. I asked one of the secretaries to call Mark and Pam at their respective work places.

Steven and I barely spoke as we drove the few blocks to the hospital. When we went into the emergency room, I gave them the necessary information and we sat down to wait. People began arriving to wait with us, Pastor Randy Davis, the administrator, the minister of music, and my friend and co-worker, Barbara. Finally, the doctor came out and said, that so far, the tests were not showing anything that would indicate a heart attack, but he was still admitting Charles for observation and more tests.

I was allowed to go back to see my husband. He was still very restless and was unable to lie down flat. He continued flexing his fingers and rubbing his arms. At some point, he said to me, "I know we are to give thanks in all things, but this is a hard one!" Shortly thereafter, he took a partially opened pack of cigarettes out of his pocket, crumpled them into a wad, and threw them across the room. I stood by quietly and watched, but did not make any comment.

In a few minutes, Mark came into the room. He wanted his dad moved to Knoxville right away, but Charles declined, saying he would stay in Morristown and see what the doctors could find. Mark was very upset, but I was accustomed to following my husband's wishes in most matters, so I told my son we would do as his father asked. Later on, I came to believe, this too, was part of God's plan.

Charles was taken to a room on the fourth floor. Two of the ministers from the church came up and waited with us. A heart monitor had been ordered; however, a long time had passed and it still had not been brought to the room. One of the men went out to the nurses' desk to find out why it had not been brought. Her response was that they had just not gotten around to doing it yet! After some conversation, it was brought to the room shortly thereafter.

I remember being out in the hallway for a brief time and coming back into the room to see Steven lying halfway on the bed with his dad, and halfway off. Charles had his arm around Steven, even with the pain he was experiencing, trying to assure his son that everything was going to be okay.

A nurse came in with a tray of food, but Charles was feeling very nauseous, and was unable to eat. He was having difficulty breathing by this time, so a respiratory therapist was sent to the room. He asked if the pain had stopped. Charles replied, that it had not, and that it was now moving down into his shoulder. The therapist immediately ordered more tests, an EKG, and blood gas tests.

The doctor returned to the room shortly after the therapist left, and gave us the unwanted news that the last tests revealed signs of heart problems. He was calling the Lifestar helicopter to air-lift Charles to Knoxville to a heart specialist. He discussed the hospital and the doctor, then left the room to make the arrangements.

Charles and I discussed it after the doctor left the room. We purposely did not mention all of the possibilities that lay before us. He did say to me, "You can just take me down in the car, can't you?" "Sure," I said. "I can take you to Knoxville in our car with you strapped to a heart monitor and an IV in your arm!" My short laugh was a bit shallow.

By this time, it was getting close to 4:00 p.m. I had sent Pam and Steven home to get some toiletries and other things we would need. Mark also had gone back home to get his vehicle since his supervisor had driven him to the hospital earlier. God's hand was at work, as none of our children were present for what came next.

I was alone in the room with Charles when he became very sick. I grabbed a small pan and held it for him. I could not reach the nurse's call button, but suddenly and miraculously, our friends, Dale and Eleanor Rose, appeared in the doorway. I asked Dale to get the nurse quickly and he ran off down the hallway.

Two nurses came hurrying into the room. They asked me to leave, so I stepped outside with Dale and Eleanor. I was only there a couple of minutes, when several people came running down the hallway toward us with their crash cart. A very kind female doctor stopped briefly to assure me they knew their jobs, and I was not to worry. How could I not worry?! As I listened to the sounds coming from that room, I turned to Eleanor and said, "He is having a heart attack in that room right now — I just know it!" And indeed, he was.

After what seemed an eternity, Charles was rolled out of the room and taken downstairs to be readied for the Lifestar helicopter. He was put in one of the cardiac rooms in the emergency area and was constantly being monitored and checked. I was called in to give permission for the administering of a new and powerful drug called a "clot buster," a drug to open the arteries. The side effects were explained and I signed the papers. Later, I wondered why it was not given when he first entered the hospital. My understanding was that it was given to prevent a heart attack. I have often contemplated if the outcome would have been different had it been administered sooner. But, all the 'what ifs' do not change anything when God's plan is in effect.

I sat in the emergency room area outside the door where their personnel continued working on Charles. Finally, I was allowed to go in to see him. He had been given some strong medication, but was trying to be quite 'chipper,' nevertheless. He pulled off his oxygen mask so I could kiss him. During all this time, he was making jokes with everyone. But, they still continued working with him. I asked a doctor if Charles had actually had a heart attack. He answered that he was in the early stages of one.

The helicopter arrived. A nurse and the pilot came in to get Charles. The emergency room doctor stopped to tell me that Charles had one of the best nurses he could have riding down with him to Knoxville. So many people were taking time to reassure me — Thank you, Lord!

They rolled Charles out into the hallway. He motioned for me to come and give him another kiss before he left. Of course, I was happy to oblige! I told him I loved him and would be following in the car. As they took him through the door toward the helicopter, I was astounded that so many of our extended family and friends had gathered. I wondered how the word had gotten out so quickly. Charles gave them a 'thumbs up' sign as he was rolled by. I remember our friends, Carolyn and Turk Burress, rushing up to me to assure me of their love and prayers. I was reminded of Turk's close call with his heart in the not too distant past.

However, I almost lost it as I watched my husband being put into that helicopter. I remember thinking, "What is ahead of us this night, God?" "It's probably going to be a long one!" But, that precious calmness kept overriding my fears and was keeping me together. "Thou wilt keep him in perfect peace whose mind is stayed on Thee." Isaiah 26:3, King James Version (KJV)

Mark brought my car around. Eleanor rode down with us. Pam and Steven rode in Amy's vehicle (Mark's wife, who was out of town). As we rode down the highway, quietly discussing the events of the day, we all thought (at least, Mark and I did) that Charles would probably have open heart surgery, a long recovery period, and would eventually be home again.

We arrived at Ft. Sanders Hospital to find many more relatives and friends already there; my mom, my sister Shirley, sister-in-law Jackie, and niece Suzanne, Clay and his wife, Betty, and so many others. Mark and I went to the business office after checking to see if there was any news on Charles. After finishing, we went back to the Intensive Care Unit (ICU) lounge to wait with everyone else.

After awhile, we were called back to the ICU to see Charles and talk with the doctor. They explained everything that was being done for him, but he was still having quite a lot of chest pain. As I walked into the room, I wanted to cry, but somewhat managed to stay calm in Charles' presence. His color was still not good. I had seen my dad a few years earlier in an ICU, but it is so different when it is your own husband!

Later on, we talked with one of the heart doctors. He too, was concerned that Charles was still having chest pain. "The only way to know what is going on in there is to just go in and find out," he told us. All of us, including Charles, agreed to a heart catheterization. When I signed the papers; however, it included any number of possibilities, including balloon procedure, or even open heart surgery. My own heart skipped a beat or two at that one!

During all of this, I was anxious, but not 'falling apart.' Perhaps, I was in denial that anything could possibly happen to MY husband! But, I also felt I had to be strong for my children, and for Charles. I realized one of the truths of being married — when one is weak, the other is strong. Charles had always been the strong one, now it was my turn to assume that role.

We went back downstairs to the ICU lounge. Since it was almost midnight, most of our friends had left to go back home. A few remained.

Some of Pam's friends had come to be with her. Steven's youth minister, Anthony Keirsey, came and took him to get something to eat. Mark, Pam, and I waited. It was probably an hour or less, but that kind of waiting can seem so very long! So many thoughts tumbled around in my head, things I should do, people I should call, etc. I remember thinking I needed to call Charles' sister, Betty, who lived in Kingsport. However, it was so late that I decided to wait until morning when I would have something more definite to tell her.

Steven returned and had not been back very long when we were summoned back upstairs again. The catheterization was completed, and Charles was back in a room. He was awake and listened to everything the doctor said. We were told he had two arteries with blockage, 75% in one, and about 80% in the other. He also drew a diagram showing where the most damage was. It was in the main pumping chamber, in the lower left side. The doctor stated nothing further should be done at this time. His statement was, "Right now, our biggest priority, is to get you through this heart attack." He went on to say, that in about six weeks, after some healing had taken place, he would then decide if something further needed to be done. Charles seemed to understand everything that was explained to us. We visited with him briefly, and then left to return to the ICU lounge and give a report to those who were still waiting. After that, they all began gathering their things to go home.

A friend and former member of our church, Alan Guy, was, at that time, the head of the Ft. Sanders Association. He had graciously arranged a room for us to use, so that we might be able to shower and have a place to sleep. This is where we were headed when we left the ICU that night. How elated we were as we walked down the hallway! Only two arteries were blocked and no surgery required! We were actually laughing, as we proceeded to our room. Later on in the evening, Mark reminded me that the doctor also said the next 48-hours were very critical. I guess in my stupor, I somehow missed that statement.

As we prepared for bed, we discussed the doctor and how impersonal he seemed, although our doctor had said he was one of the best in the area. As we talked on; however, we decided one would almost have to be impersonal to be able to deal with what the doctors and staff must see in a coronary unit every day.

It was a rough night for all of us. None of us really slept. Mark was in one bed, Pam and I were together in the other bed, and Steven laid on the floor. The events of the day kept rolling over and over in my head, as I am sure it did in theirs as well. I remember praying for Charles and asking for strength for myself and my children. Little did I know how much I was going to need every bit of strength I could muster in the hours and days ahead!

TUESDAY, AUGUST 9, 1994

"Your ship is equal to the load of today, but when you are carrying yesterday's worry and tomorrow's anxiety, you must lighten your load or you will sink."

"Forgive me, Lord, for picking up burdens I do not need to carry, and for being anxious when I forget You are in control. Thank you that I can lay this at your feet and with your help, I will not sink." ~Bless Your Heart, Series II, Heartland Samplers, Inc.

This little calendar held great significance for me during this time, because on the hardest days, it gave me comfort, as if He were there, meeting specific needs for each specific day.

I arose very early, got dressed, and went down to the ICU to check on Charles. I was told he had rested fairly well, and we could visit later on in the morning. I went back to the room upstairs, got the children up and moving, and we all went to the cafeteria to eat. I do not remember having eaten since the day before. I still could not eat very much. Worry and stress seemed to have taken my appetite away. By the time we finished eating, it was time for our first day's visit. Since only two people could go in at a time, we decided Pam and I would go first, then Mark and Steven would follow. This was at 10:30 in the morning.

My heart beat faster and faster as we walked down the hallway toward Charles' room. I was excited, but a real sense of unease filled my mind. Yet, I had to see for myself that he was okay. As we rounded the corner and started into the room, Charles was talking through his oxygen mask and raising his hands toward the ceiling. Pam asked him, "Who are you waving to, Dad?" His reply was, "I am talking to my Lord, Jesus. I feel great, I don't have pain anywhere!"

We laughed and talked. He told of his nurse apologizing that she probably had "coffee breath" as she had bent over him earlier. He had said to her, "Oh, please don't mention coffee! I would kill for a cup of coffee right now!" He said his own breath was probably horrible also. I laughed and said, "Well, at least you are the only one having to smell it with that oxygen mask over your face!" Then he proceeded to yank it off and demand a kiss! We talked on. I gently questioned him about how much he remembered of what the doctor had told us the night before. He understood he had had a heart attack and that there were two blocked arteries. That was where his memory and ours changed paths. He thought an angioplasty was going to be performed later.

Then, he began trying to use the remote control for the television. In so doing, he kept raising up his head. I could see he was getting really agitated, and he was not even supposed to be moving. I told him he needed to lie down, and I would fix it for him. He continued raising his head, this time, to get ice. Suddenly, he lay his head back and asked if there was a washcloth in the room. I found one, wet it, and put it on his forehead. His color had turned ashen. I told Pam to call the nurse. In the meantime, Charles asked me to get the pillow from under his head. He was nauseous again. The nurse appeared at that time and took his blood pressure. It had dropped considerably, and she asked us to the leave the room.

We slipped out. Pam left the unit completely, but I stayed right outside the room in the hallway. I listened and watched as he was very sick again. In fact, I don't believe I have ever seen anyone as sick as he was at that time. Two nurses came running down the hall and into the room. Then something strange happened. Charles began to just pop up into a sitting position, as though he were doing sit-ups. The nurses would push him down and he would come up again. This occurred several times. Later, I was told he was having spasms.

A huge lump began forming in my throat as I stood there and watched all that was taking place. Cold fear washed over me in waves, along with a sense of such utter helplessness. I knew his condition was very bad. The nurse came out of the room and asked me to wait outside the unit. An hour had passed since we had come to visit him.

I stepped outside of the ICU and told the children what was taking place, or as much as I knew was taking place. It seemed only a few minutes when another nurse came and escorted us all down the hallway to a small room. I knew being put in a small room meant that things had gotten very serious. She said someone would be in to talk with us very shortly.

In a matter of minutes, the nurse who was caring for Charles came in to tell us he was in cardiac arrest and probably would not make it.

There was complete silence in the room. I cried out from the very depths of my being, although no one but God heard it. My chest felt so heavy, it was as if someone had placed a huge weight on it. Dear God, this can't be happening! Not Charles, Lord! He is so young and strong and so important to your work, Lord! And I need him so much, God!

Then I looked around at my precious children, as their tears flowed silently down their cheeks. It was then that I realized they needed me – not falling apart, but strong. And the strength came. "My grace is sufficient for you, for My power is perfected in weakness." II Corinthians 12:9 (NIV).

We sat for what seemed an eternity. We discussed what we needed to do about life support. Charles had always told me and our children that he never wanted to be kept alive on machines. So, there was really no decision to make – he had already made it. Later on, I was thankful that I did not have to make that decision.

Now, 45 minutes had passed. "He's gone, Mom; he has to be, after all this time," said Mark. Then, a new doctor came to see us, a Dr. Towne. I believe God especially chose this particular doctor for Charles and for our family. He was very soft spoken, with kind eyes, and a gentle manner.

He pulled up a small chair and sat directly in front of me. He took one of my hands, and said these words,

> Mrs. Skaggs, your husband has had two simultaneous cardiac arrests, and he is in a coma at this time. We have put him on a respirator to help him breathe. He will most likely not make it. If he does, he will probably be brain-dead. He was out for over 45 minutes, and brain activity just cannot be sustained over such a long period without oxygen.

Brain-dead! Brain-dead? Oh please, God, not that! He has such a good mind! And we have to say goodbye!

Dr. Towne was still speaking, "You may take your family back to see him for a few minutes. I have called a neurologist to do a brain scan and EEG to check for any brain activity. But, I am not very hopeful since he has been experiencing spasms. This is an indicator of the lack of brain activity."

"Let him go, Mom, just let him go!" Mark cried out.

"Let's wait for the test results," I said. I was so glad we waited.

Pastor Randy and another senior staff member came, along with Ralph Wright, Pam's future father-in-law. I was so glad to see them. Pastor Randy hugged me and I told him how much I needed a hug from someone strong. We all sat down to wait again.

As we were all sitting in a circle, we began naming what Charles meant to each of us. Mark spoke up first. "He's my hero," he said. "He's my best friend," said Steven. Pam said, "I am his sweetheart." I spoke up, "I was his sweetheart first, since I was 15!" It may all seem silly now, but we were all expressing, from our hearts, just how much Charles meant to us.

Shortly after, the nurse came in and said we could go back to see Charles. What a terrible and heart-rending sight — to see my dear husband, who was always so strong and looking after others, so tied down and so dependent on machines for his very life's breath! I walked around to the far side of the bed and began telling him how much we all loved and needed him, that he was a fighter, and needed to fight this. I kissed him over and over, and begged and begged. The children were doing the same thing. I remember Steven was crying so hard and saying, "Dad, you're as stubborn as a mule! You've got to fight this thing!" Still, no response — no movement — just silence.

We stood for a few moments longer, then left, so the tests could be administered. I remember as I went into the hallway, Dr. Towne touched my arm and said, "Mrs. Skaggs, I know many prayers are being offered on behalf of your husband and we are going to do everything we can to save him." Thank you, Lord, for a doctor who knows and understands prayer.

We all went back to wait — again. Different people began to appear, some of whom the chaplain had called, and others who had just happened to be there at that time, checking on Charles. Thank goodness for Pam's friend, Heidi, who kept a list of every visit, and every phone call, that day, and the next.

As I sat looking at each of my children, I said a prayer of thanksgiving for them, that I did not have to face this alone. I also asked for added strength for each of us. I remember that I asked Pam if she would like to climb on my lap as she did when she was a little girl. She nodded through her tears and I held out my arms to her. It was a bit awkward, since she is tall and long-legged, and I am short, but, it did not matter. She needed comfort, and I needed to give it to her. I knew she would be better when her fiancé Doug arrived.

I felt really sorry for Mark. I knew he needed his wife, Amy, who was out of town, yet, he was trying to be strong, probably for my sake. She was due in that night and would be stopping at the hospital and not going on home. But, her father had come in, and I know it was helpful to Mark.

Then, there was Steven. I wondered weeks later, if I had failed him during that difficult time. He seemed to be sitting or standing by himself a few times. I motioned for Mark to go to him at one point. Also, Pastor Randy stood by him sometimes. And the youth director was also with him.

We were each struggling in our own private way to deal with what was happening. I finally got up and went out into the hallway to the restroom to be alone for a few minutes. I leaned over the sink and prayed, "God, I am not going to try and bargain with you and make promises I probably would not keep. I am simply going to ask you for a miracle. Please, God, please give him back to us. Give us a miracle, Lord. Let him live. Please restore him to health, God." And the miracles started coming, albeit not necessarily the one for which I had asked.

Over and over, I prayed this prayer and cried out to God. Then, I went back into the room with the others. Presently, the nurse came into the room and told us Charles was coming out of his coma! MIRACLE number ONE!

She also said he was responding to commands. It seems that part of the EEG test is that someone speaks very loudly into the patient's ear and calls his name. The nurse said, "I called his name in one ear, with no response." But, when I did it into the other ear, he opened his eyes and looked up at me, as if to say, "Lady, what in the world are you doing?" She wanted us all to go back to his room to see if he would respond to us.

We all trooped down the hallway and into his room. He appeared to be asleep. The nurse had said he had been given medication to keep him calm. The children gathered around his bedside, holding his hand, and speaking quietly to him. I stood back for a few minutes and just watched.

Then I said, "Let me try." Then, in a louder voice than normal, I said to him, "Hey Skaggs, wake up! This is your Honey talking!"

Those eyes instantly came wide open and searched all the faces until they came to rest on mine. I smiled at him and took his hand. I asked him to squeeze my hand, and he DID! I then turned to the nurse and said, "There is nothing wrong with this man's mind; he recognizes me!" MIRACLE number TWO!

We visited quietly for a few minutes, but he kept drifting in and out of sleep. We finally left, to give him a chance to rest and regain his strength, promising to return at the next visiting time.

Then, a lot of people began coming. There must have been at least 200 people through the hospital that day and night, to see us, and offer us their support and prayers. Pastor Randy told us all the phone lines at the church had been jammed all day because so many people were calling about him. The secretaries were unable to get anything done but answer the phones. So many people sharing their love and concern with us! And phone calls to the hospital numbered so many I could not possibly remember all of them!

Mark's wife, Amy, arrived from her trip later in the evening, and Pam's fiancé arrived from Kentucky. Neither of them realized how serious things had gotten that day, so they had to be filled in on all that information. I was really thankful they were there. Steven still looked a bit lost at times, but his youth director was there, and other friends came and went. People were there late into the night. Everyone who came was so loving and supportive to all of us. Pastor Randy, and his wife, Jeanne, were encouraging to us, and so anxious to do anything they could to help us. How thankful I was for them!

Later, staff from the preschool came and visited with me. They brought the work I was working on when this had started on Monday, because instructions were needed from me for them to finish it, and then they took it back with them. Thank you, Lord, for Barbara R., Vicki S., and Barbara B., who continued giving me their friendship and support.

I remember another friend calling to offer her support. She asked me how she should pray. I asked her to pray that I would have the grace to accept whatever God's will was for our lives. I realized, even then, that there were going to be changes; however, I suppose I was thinking in terms of an altered lifestyle, perhaps one where Charles was not able to work full-time. I just wanted, with all my being, to believe he would recover. I wondered what was going to happen next.

Charles' sister, Betty, and her son, Bill, arrived from Kingsport. I brought her up-to-date on everything that had transpired. Then, I took her back to see her brother. He was asleep, and she did not want to awaken him, so, they were unable to visit together. As we discussed later, her goodbyes to her brother had occurred three weeks earlier. One of Steven's baseball tournaments had been played in Kingsport. We had spent two days with her, more of God's hand at work, I believe. Of all the tournaments in which we had participated, none had ever been held in Kingsport! God is good!

She tried to get a room close to the hospital to spend the night but nothing was available. They did not stay too long. We promised to call if there was any change in Charles' condition.

I went down to the cafeteria with Dale and Eleanor to eat. None of us had eaten since breakfast. I was beginning to feel somewhat lightheaded from lack of sleep, no food, and tremendous stress. I remember how Dale cried as we sat and discussed all that had happened. On the previous Sunday, their family and ours had gathered at our home for Sunday dinner. As always, when we got together, we sat around telling old mission trip stories, and laughing our heads off at some of the tales. My devotional calendar for that day had read:

> "A friend is the first person who comes in when the whole world has gone out."

> "A friend loves at all times . . ." Proverbs 17:17 (NIV)

These, are the kind of friends they have always been to us. They were greatly affected by Charles' illness. I took Dale back to see him later, but they did not communicate, as Charles was asleep.

It was late. Everyone had left, and we began preparing for bed. The chairs in the ICU made into beds, so Doug, Pam, and Steven went to sleep there. Mark, Amy, and I went back to the room upstairs. Pam told me later about Steven lying there crying silent tears, and how she had gathered him in her arms, and held him until he fell asleep. I remember,

23

after going to bed, I began to shake uncontrollably. Mark assumed I was cold and brought another blanket to put over me. But I was not cold, except in my heart and spirit. He sat on the side of my bed for a long time. That act was such a blessing because I had such a great need for comfort and the nearness of someone I loved.

Wednesday, August 10, 1994

"We are shaped and fashioned by what we love." ~Goethe

". . . love the Lord your God with all your heart and with all your soul and with all your mind. This is the first and greatest commandment."

Matthew 22:37-38 (NIV)

Another night of tossing and turning came and went. We got up and dressed for another day. After breakfast, we were sitting in that same small room in the ICU when Mark said, "Mom, I wonder what we are in for today. We've been on such a roller-coaster since all this started, up one minute, and down the next." "I know, Son, but today is going to be a better day!" And yet, I was still uneasy.

We went by twos for our next visit. Pam and I went in first. Charles was awake most of the time. A different nurse was caring for him that day.

Charles kept pointing to his stomach. It took me a moment to realize he had the hiccups and it was bothering him. He began tapping his thumbs and forefingers together. We finally understood he was showing us he could not speak. It was obvious to us, because he had a respirator tube down his throat that was preventing any speech. He was very agitated and restless. We did not stay long so that Mark and Steven could visit.

I left to go back to the room upstairs to rest and to just have some quiet time before our next visit. I remembered II Corinthians 12:9, that had been tripping around in my head all day. "My grace is sufficient for you." Our Sunday school lesson the previous Sunday was entitled, "Strength In Weakness." That Scripture and lesson were just what I needed at this particular time in my life. What a wonderful God we have! This verse reminded me that He supplies everything we need, sometimes before we are even aware that we need it!

As I lay on the bed in the quietness of that room, I could not sleep. My heart and mind were filled with gratitude as I thought of all God had done for us during the past 48 hours, of all the people He had sent to minister to us, of the particular needs He had met, and that Charles was still alive. I am not a very demonstrative person when it comes to worship, but at that particular moment in my life, I just had to raise my hands and praise God. I felt that the Holy Spirit was surrounding me with His love at that moment. "Father, please give me the grace to praise you in all circumstances — not to question your wisdom or to grow bitter. It is so difficult, especially when uncertainty plagues my path."

Shortly after, I went downstairs for our second visit. Steven and I went in together this time. Charles was more alert and more like himself. As soon as he saw me enter the room, he puckered his lips and motioned me over for a kiss. Of course, I was more than happy to do so! On our last visit, I had pulled an IV tube loose trying to get close enough to kiss him! Needless to say, I was more careful this time! Once, when the nurse asked us to step out of the room for a few minutes, Charles quickly pointed his finger at her. She laughed, and assured him I would be allowed right back in shortly.

Charles had been biting down on the respirator tube. Each time he did, it set off an alarm. It was cutting off the very air he needed to breathe. They had put a clamp of some sort in his mouth to prevent this from happening. He kept trying to push it out of his mouth with his tongue and motioning for water. The nurse explained why he could not have water. But she did tell him she would remove the clamp and swab his mouth if he promised he would stop biting down on the tube. He nodded his agreement. After she finished and left the room, I gently chided him. I reminded him all these people were here to help him and he was going to have to cooperate to get well. He became calmer after that.

Steven was standing near the foot of the bed. He told Charles, "I don't want you to worry about us, Dad; we are all okay. We just want you to do what they tell you and get well." Assurances from a 14-year-old! Then, Steven looked over at me. As he did so, Charles tapped him with his foot. When Steven looked back at him, Charles pointed first to Steven, and then to me. Both Steven and I knew what he was doing. He was telling his son to take care of his mom. Even in his condition, he was thinking about my welfare. Or perhaps, he knew something the rest of us had not yet grasped. What strong love and devotion he had for his family!

The others had their visit. I went downstairs with Pam, Doug, and Steven to the lounge. Mark and Amy went upstairs to rest. Around 3:00

p.m., someone called to check on Charles. I was giving them a report when suddenly Mark ran breathlessly into the room. "He's in trouble again, Mom! Let's go!" I hung up the phone, got the others, and we ran to the elevator. On the way up, Mark explained that his blood pressure was fluctuating a great deal, and his heartbeat was very erratic. We went back to the ICU and were taken to another small room.

This time, I knew deep in my heart, he was either already gone, or he was not going to make it. As we sat there in that room, I began shivering, but again, not from being cold. It came from an ache that was starting in the deepest part of me. I prayed silently. As we waited, there was no conversation. I believe we all realized the same thing, but no one wanted to voice it. The tears that were shed, fell silently. The chaplain had been notified, and calls were already been made. I knew Pastor Randy was on the way.

After awhile, Dr. Towne came into the room and sat down across from me. He explained that Charles' heart had stopped again, and they had to use electrogenic shock to get it pumping again. He had sustained such massive damage in the main pumping chamber during the original attack that his heart just could not pump enough blood to keep him going. He further explained that 90% of people with this kind of damage would not make it at all. The other 10% lived the rest of their lives in bed, or in a wheelchair. He was going to perform another test to measure blood flow into his heart.

Before he left the room; however, he asked if Charles had a living will. I said he did not. But, I assured him of Charles' wishes, that he had expressed to me and to our children on many occasions, that he didn't ever want to be kept alive on machines. The doctor, knowing the difficulty of making a decision that would end my husband's life, reminded us we also needed to consider the quality of life Charles would have.

The terrible sadness began to permeate my whole being, a sadness that still appears on occasion, even today, a sadness that seemed to underlie my every thought and action, even the laughter that eventually returned. The tears fell as we sat there trying to process all that was happening. But, we all agreed what we had to tell the doctor when he returned.

Pastor Randy arrived. As was his usual action, he hugged me. He spoke very little. I was so glad to see him. When you have someone like Charles to lean on for 29 years, someone with quiet strength in time of crisis, someone you trust completely, it is very difficult to find yourself in the position of having to be the strong one. It is very ironic — Charles was the one I wanted and needed the most, yet, he could not help us. Other family members and friends came. We all waited, something we had been doing often the last few days.

Dr. Towne came into the room again. He sat with me and gently explained again, that Charles' heart could only continue beating by been shocked, and that we needed again to consider the quality of life he would have. There really was no decision to make. "I know my husband's wishes," I told him. "From what he has told the children and me many times, we know he would not want to be kept alive this way."

"Okay, Mrs. Skaggs. We will get him ready, and your family can go back to spend the rest of the time with him." He explained what would happen at the end, patted my hand, and left the room. The young nurse appeared at the door a few minutes later to tell us we could go back to be with him. She was crying so hard she could hardly speak. I got up and went over to her and put my arms around her in an effort to give her some measure of comfort.

Without a word, everyone cleared out of the room, leaving me alone with my family. We spontaneously gathered in a circle of love with our arms around each other as I prayed. I asked God for His strength and peace for the days ahead, and that He would gently usher Charles into heaven. I praised Him and asked that we would be positive witnesses, and that He would receive honor through all of this. When the prayer was finished, I said to the children, "Now kids, I want us all to get our faces straightened up before we go in to be with Dad. I don't want us going in there crying and upset and having him worried about us." And we were able to do just that! MIRACLE number THREE!

We walked, for the last time, down the hallway, and into the room where my husband lay. As I went up to the bedside and took his hand, I was struck by the overwhelming peace on his face and the gentleness of his countenance. He had the same incredible peace I was feeling in my own spirit at that very moment. Pastor Randy commented later, he believed Charles had caught a glimpse of heaven when he had the last cardiac arrest. I agreed.

Charles saw Pastor Randy standing off to the side and motioned him closer. He mouthed the word, "Pray." He took Charles' hand and prayed a beautiful prayer. When he finished, Charles mouthed the words, "I love you." Pastor Randy responded in kind. I had asked the nurse, upon entering the room, if the respirator could be removed so he could communicate with us, but she said it would only make it more difficult for him in the end.

So we each, in turn, told our husband, father, father-in-law, and friend, how much we loved him. I kissed him several times and held his hand close to my heart. When I would start to release it and lay it on the bed, he would hold it even more firmly. All the while, we were casting glances at the blood pressure machine. The doctor had told us his pressure would continue to drop until there was no more.

I bent over him and asked, "Charles, are you totally at peace?" He looked up at me with a look of surprise, as if to say, "How could you even ask?" Then, with that twinkle in his eye that I knew so well, he nodded his head and winked at me. In that one brief moment, we connected in that way that only a husband and wife can possibly know; and I knew, without any doubt, that all was well with Charles Skaggs — in this life, or the next! Thank you, Father!

As he began to get weaker, I put my arms around him as best as I could, with all the wires and other obstructions that were keeping me from him. I wanted so much to be able to pull him up against me and hold him as tightly as I could, or just to lie down beside him and hold him. Instead, I could do nothing but hold his hand and watch as life was slowly leaving his body.

After a few moments, he pushed back with his shoulders.

I knew the end was near. Time for me stood still.

I was unaware of nothing but his face.

My precious husband was slipping away from me, and I could not bear the thought of letting him go.

"Goodbye, Dad, I'll see you soon," Mark said. The others said their goodbyes as well. I watched as his eyes slowly started to roll back in his head. "That's it, Mom, let's go," said Mark.

"No, wait," I said. Charles eyes had come back down at the sound of Mark's voice and he looked at me one more time. I felt that he saw me, but I am not sure. At this point, he was already heaven-bound! His eyes went back to rest in a glassy stare toward the ceiling.

"It's time to go, Mom," the children told me. I did not want to leave, but I knew it was time. Pastor Randy stayed with Charles a few minutes after we left.

We walked out into the hallway and watched a few minutes on the monitor. There was no more movement. We went back to the same room where we had been before. Pastor Randy followed shortly thereafter. He held me while I cried. Suddenly, I no longer felt like a whole person, but as if somehow, half of me had been violently stripped away. My heart was racing, my hands trembled, and it was hard to breathe.

We went back to see Charles before they took him away. It was amazing! His head was turned slightly toward the door as if he were expecting us. He looked so peaceful as I bent to kiss him once more. His face was still warm but the coldness of death was very much in his hands.

Outside the room, I held each of my sons, and told them I did not expect them to try to take their father's place. I was especially concerned for Steven, since his dad had indicated he wanted Steven to take care of me. He was trying to be so brave, telling everyone that everything was going to be okay, when his own heart was breaking. Family members and others were in the waiting area down the hall when we came out. My sister, Shirley, and her husband, Buddy were there, along with my mother. They had come, not because they had been told of new problems, but simply from a strong sense that something was wrong. Later, Shirley told me how hard Buddy cried on the way home from the hospital that day. We had spent a lot of time with them over the years. My brother, Neill, and my sister-in-law, Jackie, were also there, and my friend, Eleanor.

At some point, I went into what I call 'automatic pilot.' It had probably begun days before; I just had not realized it. It is what happens when the hurt is so deep, the pain so intense; yet, you are still able to function on some level. Many times in prior months, I had lain awake crying into my pillow as I lay beside my husband, imagining this very thing happening, losing him, and thinking I would not be able to bear it. Isn't it strange that I would have had such thoughts! Perhaps it was a part of God's preparation for this time in my life. But, no one can ever imagine the pain could be so deep, or the loss so devastating to one's very soul.

I went to the nurses and thanked them for all they had done for Charles, and how they had fought for him using all their skills. They had treated him and our family with much kindness and compassion. I gave them information for removal of his body and signed the necessary papers. Then, we prepared to leave. I remember as I got into the car, Tom W., a friend and former church member, came running across the parking lot to tell me how sorry he was, with his own tears flowing freely.

As we started the long journey home, Pam became the "mother," and held me this time as I sat there and cried on her shoulder. She held Steven part of the time as well. During those three hospital days, and long afterward, I was constantly surprised and pleased at the maturity I saw developing in her. She was, and is, a constant source of comfort and strength to me.

I also saw the maturity and responsibility in Mark as he helped me make decisions, very much the same way his father would have done. Charles may have gone on to heaven, but so much of him is still with me in our children. Yes, we are 'shaped and fashioned by what we love.'

As we came into Morristown and the steeple of First Baptist Church first appeared, we all began to tear up again. This church was like a second home to Charles. He had invested not just time over the years, but so much of his heart, his very self, into ministry there.

We came up our street and home was in view. Home — what an inviting word, a word that denotes family, warmth, comfort, security, protection, and hope for the future. But for me, at this moment, I felt nothing but a dread at having to enter our home with the knowledge that Charles would never again be there. My heart was pounding as we pulled into the carport. The street and driveway were lined with cars and people waiting to see us. I told Mark to tell everyone that I just had to have a few minutes alone before I could speak with anyone. He did so, and I slipped through the back of the house to our bedroom alone and closed the door.

I lay down on the bed and poured out my tears. I simply could not imagine never having his warmth beside me anymore in this room, where we had shared our love, our secrets, our laughter, and yes even a fight or two! Presently, I heard movement at the door. I looked up and saw Mark standing there right outside the door. I motioned for him to come in. He came and lay beside me and held me for a long time. Eventually, the other two children came drifting in, one-by-one, and got on the bed with me.

We began talking about what Charles would say had he walked into the room and seen us. He would have said in his gruffest voice, "What's going on in here?!" Then he would have piled on top of us! We all laughed. Yes, we were able to laugh even through our sorrow as we remembered. What a gift laughter is! "A cheerful heart is good medicine . . ." Proverbs 17:22 NIV

We talked about the children's childhood, that every Saturday morning they would come running into the bedroom, jump on the bed with us, and start wrestling with their dad. I would be yelling for them to stop, of course, but laughing right along with them. Amy said, "If you have these kinds of memories of your daddy, you are truly blessed." And we were. And we still are.

We got up after awhile and went out to see the people who had come. So many came, bringing food and other items to help us, and expressing their own grief at our loss and theirs. How blessed we were to have so many wonderful, caring friends!

People stayed at the house until very late. After everyone left, we all sat down in the living room to decide what we wanted to do. At age 48, planning a funeral for my husband was certainly not what I wanted to be doing, but it had to be done. We planned the funeral for the next evening at the church (where else could it be?), with the burial on Friday morning at 11:00 a.m. We collectively wrote an obituary for the newspaper and selected a picture to go with it.

We all went to bed late, our little family of six now, instead of seven, diminished by the loss of the one, yet strengthened with each other through that same loss. Pam slept with me, Mark and Amy were in Pam's room, and Doug and Steven were in Steven's room. I remember shaking uncontrollably again as had happened in the hospital. Pam held me until it passed.

Oh, the darkness of that first night, the overwhelming sadness and loneliness! Even a sleeping pill did not work. I had to just endure the night until morning came. This was the beginning of many nights of "just enduring." Yet somewhere in my mind, was the knowledge that "The Lord is close to the brokenhearted . . ." Psalm 34:18 (NIV).

Thursday, August 11, 1994

"Closer is He than breathing, and nearer than hands and feet."
~Alfred Lord Tennyson

"You make known to me the path of life; you will fill me
with joy in your presence, with eternal pleasures at your right
hand." Psalm 16:11 (NIV)

The light of dawn came early. How thankful I was! When I first
awoke, for a few seconds it seemed like any ordinary summer morning.
Then I looked over and saw Pam asleep beside me. Then, I was assaulted
again by the tremendous pain.

I lay there a few minutes, listening to the stillness of the house,
realizing no one else was up yet. I got up, dressed, and carried my Bible
and a glass of juice out to the front porch, as I did many mornings.
There is something so refreshing about the stillness of an early summer
morning. I read Psalm 84. I knew this was a Scripture I wanted to be read
at Charles' funeral. "I would rather be a doorkeeper in the house of my
God than to stand in the courts of the wicked." How appropriate for a
man who had given so much time and effort to our church!

Mark came out and sat for a few minutes. I remember telling him how
sorry I was for all the times I had fussed at Charles over little things that
did not matter. "Little things is all that they were then, and that's all they
are now, Mom," said Mark. "Dad knew how much you loved him, so don't
worry about those little things now." His words were some of his father's
own common sense wisdom coming through!

Later in the morning, we went to the funeral home to take Charles'
clothes, and select a casket. They all looked so cold! Mark and I both
spotted one made of a beautiful wood that looked so much warmer
than all the others. It was simple and sturdy, but beautiful, like Charles.
"Remember what Dad always said, Mom," said Mark, "Just put me in a
pine box and drop me in the ground!" The family all agreed, so that is
the one we chose.

We finished with all the details and started back home. My friend,

Carolyn B., caught us outside to tell me she had an emergency in Kentucky and would not be at the funeral, but she gave me a verse. "Precious in the site of the Lord is the death of his faithful servants." Psalm 116:15 (NIV). Amen to that!

People were in and out of the house all day. Several of my friends came and stayed to take care of feeding everyone and meeting the needs of my family. I have a very large family; we were all so grateful for all the wonderful food that poured in during those three days.

Pastor Randy came over later to discuss the funeral service. I told him I wanted a service of praise and worship and a celebration for the life of this special man. I also shared with him some details about Charles and his service in our church down through the years, since Pastor Randy was a fairly new pastor, and had not been in our church very long. He wrote down many notes.

When we finished our conversation, he asked the children to come into the room. He spoke quietly to them of the wonderful legacy their father had left them, a legacy of love and faithfulness to our family, our church, and a legacy of service. He then turned to Pam and told her he knew how much it was going to hurt, not having her daddy to walk her down the aisle on her wedding day that was coming up in March. "But, keep this thought in mind, Pam," he said, "Someday your daddy is going to escort you down the aisles of heaven." Thank you, Lord, for a pastor with a sensitive heart.

Later in the day, I was lying down trying to get some rest and Steven came into the room. He lay down with me, and held me for some time. Then, he reminded me what I had told him a few months back, that I believed God had something special in mind for him, because of the circumstances of his birth, and how we had almost lost him.

Steven said, "Mom, I think I've figured out what that special thing is — it is to take care of my mom." What a load for a 14-year-old boy to carry! I reminded him again that he could not, and should not, expect to fill his dad's shoes; that we were going to take care of each other.

In the afternoon, we went to the funeral home to view Charles' body. A huge lump came into my throat as I walked into that room. I was carrying two plaques in my hands to place in the casket for the service. They were those honoring him for his years of service in the television ministry of our church. I had asked the children to allow me a few minutes alone with him. As I started down that long room, with his body at the other hand, I found myself running to get to him! I bent over his body to kiss him. His body was so cold! There is nothing so cold as the coldness of death! It is a terrible thing to feel that coldness when only the day before, there was warmth in the touch of his hand.

Time quickly passed and 5:30 p.m. came quickly. We were to start receiving friends at 6:00. As we came up Main Street in front of the funeral home, there in a line, were all the boys on Steven's Babe Ruth All-Star baseball team, and their coaches, to support him and our family. Steven began to cry. We had shared many summers with all these boys and their parents.

We drove on to the parking lot of the church and got out of the car. We had purchased a wreath of greenery, and Mark and Amy went upstairs to place it on the front of the sound board. This was appropriate since most of Charles' time in the television ministry had been spent operating the sound system in the sanctuary. The wreath remained there for many months. No one wanted to be the one to take it down. The men from the funeral home were in the church foyer. Pastor Randy and Jeanne were down front with the casket. I went up to the casket, leaned over it, and said, "Honey, we're going to send you home in style!" Of course, nothing we did could compare with being escorted by God's angels through the gates of heaven! We were told where to stand and the people began coming.

I had never seen such an outpouring of love as we received from our church and community that night! We stood in the receiving line for three hours, as one-by-one, people came to express their sorrow and share in our grief – adult men, many of whom had worked with Charles over the years, men with tears in their eyes, women sobbing, and little children hugging us. We found ourselves in the role of comforter rather than being comforted. And that was as it should be. About halfway through, the funeral director asked if I wanted to stop the receiving line. But, I believed that if people cared enough to come, we should speak with each one — and we did.

The service began sometime after 9:00 p.m. The church was almost full. All of the church staff were on the left side; Higher Ground Ministry team was on the right side; and about 40 deacons were seated behind us as honorary pallbearers. I tried not to look at that closed casket. In the voice of everyone who spoke, prayed, or sang, the emotion was evident. Jim Mathis prayed a beautiful opening prayer, speaking of how Charles had left his footprint in every area of the church; Gene North sang, "How Great Thou Art," which was Charles' favorite hymn, and our good friend, Dale Rose, spoke with humor and emotion of his friend Charles.

Then, Pastor Randy gave a beautiful and uplifting sermon on Charles as a father. He spoke of his faithfulness, commitment, and love for God, his family, and his church. I had always known what a fine man Charles was and how much he had contributed, and now, many others would know as well. I was thankful for that. We were reminded of the fullness of joy he was now experiencing as the pastor spoke of angels having escorted him into heaven the night before.

What sustaining grace God gives! I sat there without tears, and I smiled my encouragement to each one who participated in the service. Then, it was over. Danny Georges prayed the final prayer, and everyone stood up to leave. We followed his body, as it was rolled out of the sanctuary, the last time he would ever be there in the place that he knew and loved so well. The piano and organ swelled with the sounds of the beautiful song, "Great is Thy Faithfulness" as we walked out.

In the foyer, I hugged Dale and thanked him for his wonderful words about Charles. I thanked Pastor Randy for being a friend, as well as a pastor. Then, Jim M. whisked us out the back door before we ended up in another receiving line. I understand there had been more people who had come but had not been able to speak with us. I felt badly about that, but we were all exhausted, and needed to go home. We had another hard day ahead of us the next day.

At the house, there were more people, mostly family and close friends. Food was plentiful and was put out for everyone. After they all left, we again piled on someone's bed and talked, laughed, and cried as we reminisced. The time was late again, as we just could not seem to part with each other. We drew strength from being together. Yet, tomorrow was another day to face, and we all needed rest.

Friday, August 12, 1994

". . . be content with what you have, because God has said;
Never will I leave you;
Never will I forsake you."
Hebrews 13:5 (NIV)

We were up and about early, eating and getting dressed. We drove to the funeral home for the final viewing of Charles' body. As I walked up to the casket and looked at my husband, I thought again what a handsome man he was, even with his gray hair. I had always been proud of his good looks and neatness. I told him how much I loved him and how blessed I had been that we had been together so long, almost 29 years. I knew, of course, that he was not hearing me. This was just the shell of the person I had known and loved. I knew he was with God, but this was the face and body that was as familiar to me as my own. How hard it is to say goodbye in this life, even though you know it is not the end. But, death and parting are as much a part of life as living.

I moved back and Mark and Amy went up to the casket. Mark stuck a piece of black fabric in his dad's lapel. He had asked me about it earlier. It was a piece of his graduation gown from Tennessee Tech University. Charles had not gone to college, and he was so proud of Mark for getting his education. Of course, I did not mind this gesture.

Pam and Doug went up next. Daddy's "little girl" no longer had her daddy. No matter how old you are, when you lose a loving father, you never stop being that little girl. I understood what she was feeling. I had felt the same way when my father died five years earlier. I was thankful Doug was there for her.

Then, Steven walked slowly up to the casket. He went alone, but I felt he wanted to be. My eyes filled again as I watched him speak to his dad and his best friend. Then he laid on Charles' arm the medal he had received at the baseball tournament two weeks earlier. He and Charles had shared many hours on the baseball fields. My own heart was breaking all over again as I witnessed my children's grief.

Other family members said their goodbyes, and then we got into our cars for the ride to the cemetery. My breath caught and the shaking began as I listened to the slamming of the door to the hearse. We slowly pulled out of the parking lot. Amy took my hand and squeezed it tightly all the way to the cemetery.

The service there was brief but very moving. Our youth director prayed; Pastor Randy read scripture and spoke a few words; and Clay K., our longtime friend, came and stood with his hand on my shoulder while he prayed the closing prayer. Then, it was over. Little did I know that the real pain had not yet even begun, as there were going to be adjustments to make, of which, I was not even aware!

Afterwards, we spoke to many of the people who had come for the service, and it was time to go. I turned and looked one last time at that wooden casket with the beautiful coral roses on top.

Back at the house there were many people milling about and eating. I appreciated their presence, but I must admit, I was glad they did not stay long. Betty, her son, Bill, and his wife, Sue, got ready to leave. I felt very badly that I had not gotten to spend much time with them. But there were just so many people around me all the time. Yet I knew Betty was really hurting. She had lost her little brother. I said goodbye to them and they left.

We were all exhausted and tried to get some rest. Later on in the day we went back to the cemetery gravesite. It all seemed so unreal to me. At some level of consciousness, I did feel a measure of peace and joy; however, on another level, was the feeling that this was all just a bad dream, and I would soon wake up and find it had all gone away. Even many months later, I still felt shock when I thought of his being gone and never coming back to us.

Later that night, Mark began speaking with me about my financial situation. I suppose I was dealing with so much on an emotional level in handling the grief, I had not had time to consider that my life might, out of necessity, have to change. That was another shock to my senses! I suddenly realized my income, because of Charles's death, was only about 20% of what it had been before. We discussed some possibilities and made arrangements to talk with my brother, Neill, the next day.

I remember praying when I went to bed that night, that I would trust the Father for my needs and those of my children. How many times it seems we pray words, but when we are really put to the test, this is when they begin to really mean something in our lives. We find out if we really believe words like 'faith' and 'trust.' I know I was trying with all my heart to believe them!

Saturday, August 13, 1994

"Forget the former things; do not dwell on the past. See, I am doing a new thing! . . ." Isaiah 43:18-19 (NIV)

We were all really slow in getting moving. I was feeling very bad physically, but Mark and I got ready and went to talk to my brother. We spent a long time with him and made some plans. He told me the things I needed to take care of first thing Monday morning.

Back home, Steven brought a tape recorder into my bedroom. He wanted me to hear a song recorded by *Truth*, a contemporary group. These were the words;

My prayers have all been answered; I've finally arrived.
The healing that had been delayed has now been realized.
No one's in a hurry, there's no schedule to keep;
We're all enjoying Jesus, just sitting at his feet.

My light and temporary trials have worked out for my good,
To know it brought Him glory when I misunderstood.
Though we've had our sorrows, they can never compare.
What Jesus has in store for us no language can share.

Chorus:
If you could see me now, I'm walking streets of gold.
If you could see me now, I'm standing tall and whole.
If you could see me now, you know I've seen His face.
If you could see me now, you know the pain's erased.
You wouldn't want me to ever leave this perfect place.
If you could only see me now.

~Kim Noblitt, BMI Integrity Music, 1994

As I sat listening to these words, of course, my tears spilled over again. It was as if Charles himself were speaking to me, telling me that everything was okay, that heaven was so much more than the human mind can fathom. Later on the next week; however, I listened again. The

41

realization suddenly came to me that God <u>had</u> answered my prayer that day in the hospital restroom. The second line that read, "The healing that had been delayed has now been realized," helped me understand. I had asked for healing and restoration of health for my husband. How much more restored and healed could Charles be than he was in heaven?

People continued to come and go, so the day went by quickly. By evening, I was feeling really badly, so Mark called Dr. Barclay, our family doctor, who personally came by with some medication. We went to bed late, with plans to attend the Sunday church service the next day. I really dreaded going back that first time since the funeral, but I knew it was something we all had to face. Also, I felt we needed to witness to others that you <u>can</u>, with God's help, survive such a trauma in the life of a family.

Sunday, August 14, 1994

"Our duty is not to see through one another, but to see one another through."

"Carry each other's burdens, and in this way you fulfill the law of Christ." Galatians 6:2 (NIV)

I cannot truly put into words how extremely difficult it was to walk into the sanctuary of First Baptist Church on Sunday morning after Charles' body had lain there on Thursday night! It is almost impossible to fully describe the gamut of emotions that went through my senses. I was then, and still am, drawn to that place because of the support and comfort I feel there; however, it is bittersweet. There was so much of Charles there. Everywhere I looked, I was reminded of him in some way.

The service was almost another memorial and tribute to Charles. My thoughts kept drifting in and out during the sermon; but one thing really stood out to me. It was when Pastor Randy spoke of the imminent return of Christ. I felt such a strong sense of this, stronger than I ever had before. "Forgive me, Lord, right now, heaven means being reunited with Charles more than being with you. I pray you know this is my grief talking!"

We ate lunch with the North family that day. They are such a sweet family, especially Sherry. She has such a genuine servant heart, more than most people I have known. I became ill toward the end of the meal, and she made me lie down and pampered me as if I were a child. We left shortly to return back home. At this point, I was able to handle things pretty well, because all the children were still staying at the house. But that too, was getting ready to change.

It began late that afternoon. Doug left to go back to Kentucky, where he was working at the time. Then, Pam left to go out with some of her friends. Then, Steven left with Anthony, his youth director, who had stood by him so much. I knew the time had come for Mark and Amy to return to their house and get back to their own lives. I hugged them and said my goodbyes, then came back into my home, alone for the first time since Charles had died. Even today, I still remember the terrible pain of the grief I felt, and the pain of aloneness, so strong it was almost like a physical pain. I walked through the empty house, crying out in my despair and loneliness. Finally, I could stand it no longer. I got into Charles' truck and went driving, with no destination. I just knew I had to get out of that house. I drove around awhile and came back home, a home that was now so empty without Charles.

I did not go to bed until Pam and Steven were back home. The need to draw them in around me and to protect was very strong. Part of it was the 'mother hen' instinct that all mothers seem to have, but another part was that feeling of total responsibility for them. Yet Pam was a young woman preparing to 'leave the nest' and begin her life with Doug. And Steven was at the age of being a child/man, where he was neither a child, nor a man, but some of both. He did not think he needed mothering, but contrary to what he thought, I knew he was not ready for adult responsibilities.

Well, tomorrow was another day to face. I was reminded of another song with a particular line that says, "One day at a time, sweet Jesus, that's all I'm asking of you," and that is all that I asked — strength for each day, one day at a time.

MONDAY, AUGUST 15, 1994

"The blue of heaven is larger than the darkness of the clouds.

When we see the lilies spinning in distress,
Taking no thought to manufacture loveliness,
When we see the birds all building barns for store,
'Twill be the time for us to worry, not before.

Be still, my anxious heart. . ."

~L. B. Cowman

Monday was a very dark and gloomy day, a day that matched my own spirit. Neill had instructed me to go to the Social Security Office, first thing, to take care of getting benefits for Steven and me. How I dreaded that! But Kathy, my nephew's wife who worked there, called me very early at home, and told me exactly what information and papers I would need to bring.

Beginning with her, God placed people in my path all day, to help me in the special ways I needed help. She was there to meet me when I arrived and stayed with me until I was called back to handle my affairs. She had requested a lady to help me whom she felt was one of the best there.

I struggled to hold back the tears, but the benefits were more than I had anticipated. I could hold them back no longer when I reached my car. As I turned on the ignition, a song was coming over the radio with these words, ". . . be not dismayed, what 'ere betide; God will take care of you." He constantly reminded me of His love and care, and continues to do so even today, many years later.

I drove to the bank to change the names on our accounts. As I walked in and looked at the tellers, all of whom were busy at the time, I remembered one in particular who had never seemed very friendly, who was so business-like. 'Please don't let her be the one to help me,' I thought. But, she was the very one who finished first and turned to assist me. Once again, God knew my needs and met them. She turned out to be a most kind and helpful lady, and continued to be every time I was in the bank. But for the first time, I had to say out loud, "My husband has passed away." So painful!

Later in the day, Pastor Randy brought his daughter and a friend over with something for Steven. He asked me how I was doing, <u>really</u> doing. I told him I was "hanging in" as best I could. Then, he said something I have often had occasion to remember. He looked straight at me and said these words, "Peggy, you don't always have to be a positive witness. At some point, you are going to have to let down a little, perhaps even to the point of getting angry with God. And that's okay too, because He knows that it is not your normal spirit toward Him."

As I have stated before, God has always known my exact needs and provided for them every time. That statement from Pastor Randy freed me to grieve as I needed to grieve, totally and completely. I suppose I had been operating under the premise that I had to be the strong one for everyone else, to the point that it was affecting me, not only mentally and emotionally, but physically as well.

That night, I began to let down. I cried long and hard before falling into a fitful sleep. I woke up around 2:00 a.m. with a feeling of absolute terror in my heart. Where are you, Charles? O God, he's not here, and he will never be here again! I turned on the television to the Christian network just to hear some music or anything to take away the fear. I knew in my heart that God was there with me, but I felt as if I were drowning in a sea of sorrow, and I was fearful that I would not be able to get out of it.

Tuesday, August 16, 1994

"Do not be anxious about anything, but in every situation, by prayer and petition, with thanksgiving, present your requests to God. And the peace of God, which transcends all understanding, will guard your hearts and your minds in Christ Jesus." Philippians 4:6 (NIV)

How I was to need that verse later on in the day! I was at the hospital early to have some tests run to see what was causing the pain I was having. Mark insisted on going with me, against my objections, but secretly, I was glad he was there!

Later in the day, the sky got cloudy with a pending storm. There was a storm raging in my midsection as well. By that time, I was drawn up in pain; I thought I was having a gallbladder attack. My friend and neighbor, sweet Sandy Kelly, came over later to check on me. I think the children were frightened and may have called her. The rain was pouring outside, and I was miserable.

I asked Pam if she would sleep with me again. I was crying, of course. I told her it was not that I was afraid of having surgery, if they were gallstones; it was just that I was at such a low point, I didn't know if I could handle anything else major in my life. And I really needed Charles to be with me!

The next day, I did not even want to get out of bed. I was just so physically and emotionally drained. I lay there reading my Bible and some of the huge stack of notes and cards I had received. Later on that afternoon, the doctor called and said that my problem could be treated with medication. There was our marvelous Lord, taking care of my problems again!

Karen Rose, daughter of Dale and Eleanor, came by later in the day. She sat beside me with tears in her eyes as she recounted something that had happened with her the day Charles died. On that day, she was in Africa, waiting on a train to take her group to an airport for their return trip home. She said she suddenly felt such a weight of unexplainable sadness that she began to cry. Later on, she told her mother on her last night at home, that she and Charles had visited together for a long time at the Rose house the last time we were there. She tearfully stated she had a strong sense when she left for Africa the next day someone would not be there when she returned — she just did not know who it would be.

According to Scripture, we are not to be anxious about tomorrow. Usually the things we worry about never happen anyway. Yet, I believe I had known for some time Charles and I would not grow old together. Perhaps it was intuition or God was preparing me.

Some of Those "First" Days

The days that followed were sometimes clear; more often, one day ran into the next. I know there were days that I was still operating automatically, because I was unable to recall things I had said or done. There were so many 'firsts' you have to go through that first year. Our wedding anniversary was one of those 'firsts.'

> "It is helpful to make a habit of offering, morning by morning, the troubles of the day to our Lord, accepting His will in all things, especially in all the little personal trials and vexations."
> ~H. L. Lear

> "Though I walk in the midst of trouble, You preserve my life. . . ."
> Psalm 138:7 (NIV)

How I dreaded October 12th, our wedding anniversary! Twenty-nine years of married life had come to an end. We had made our vows to love each other until death parted us, and that is just what we did; however, as with most of the 'firsts,' the anticipation of the day is probably much worse than the actual day. My perception is that family and friends are really praying for you on the actual day, but perhaps they do not think about it so much on the prior days leading up to that special day.

Pastor Randy had called earlier in the week to see if I would sing in a revival he was conducting on Thursday night. I could not even discuss it without crying. He understood, gave me some encouraging words, and prayed before we ended the conversation.

Two of my teachers, Barbara and Vicki, took me to lunch that day so I would not be alone that afternoon. Later that evening in bed, I allowed myself to remember past anniversaries, especially the last one we had celebrated the year before. We had spent the night in Gatlinburg, and I had done some little things to make the night more special. As I thought back on the evening, I was so thankful we had that time alone together. It took so little to make Charles happy!

I remembered how we sometimes held hands when we were out somewhere, like teenagers! With our children growing up and 'leaving the nest,' we were starting to recapture some of the romance of earlier years. It was a wonderful feeling! Or perhaps God was giving me some special memory to hang on to during this time in my life. How I was starting to miss that, and the sense of feeling cute, and special, and protected by someone you love. I really began to understand the saying, that we do not truly appreciate what we have until we lose it.

Birthdays were equally as difficult. Pam's was first, October 18th. Mark was out of town, so Pam, Steven, Amy, and I had dinner together at home. On Steven's birthday, the next of the 'firsts,' November 6th, he came into my room, tears streaming down his face, carrying the baseball bat his father had bought for him back in the summer. I remember it was quite expensive, so we had told him it would be an early birthday gift. Pam heard us and came in to sit down beside me on the bed. She put her arm around her little brother and said, "It's okay to cry, Steven; I cried on my birthday, too."

Steven began playing football right after school started. In October, he broke his arm. On the way to the emergency room, I remember that he looked up to the sky and said, "Dad, I bet you're getting a good laugh out of this!" We had all teased him because he seemed to get hurt so often. However, we were not laughing the next day. It was pouring rain, and I had to take him to Knoxville and try to find a doctor's office in an area I had never driven before. I remember as I was going to pick up his x-rays at the local hospital before driving to Knoxville, I felt so angry at Charles for not being here when I needed him. It was really the only time I felt any anger at all.

Thanksgiving came and went with less difficulty than I had anticipated. We spent part of the day with my siblings and family at my brother, Glenn's house. Then the kids and I went on to Mark and Amy's house later that evening.

As soon as Thanksgiving had passed, I began bracing myself for the Christmas season. I knew this one would be much harder. I got really busy and involved with the preschool. But, when the time came to decorate the house, I could not bear the thoughts of it. Each family has its own traditions for the holidays, and we were no exception. I realized our traditions would, of necessity, have to change. One of those traditions was, that we would all pile into the old Ford station wagon, (which the children had dubbed, the 'bat mobile') and we would go off to some lot to purchase our own special tree. Charles was the one who always strung the lights on the tree. Then, he would lie on the floor watching as the children and I did the rest.

Pam and I did go and get a tree. We all three struggled to get it into a tree stand, but the decorating would not have taken place if Pam had not taken over. I was so tired from the stress, lack of sleep, and my emotions, that I finally went to talk with Pastor Randy. He listened to me for about two hours; I do not believe I could have gone on without having talked to him that day. He gave me some much needed encouragement and support.

One thing that occupied my thoughts that Christmas was, that Pam and I began making preparations for her wedding day to be held on March 25th of the upcoming year. It was a good detractor for the thoughts and memories that threatened to overtake me during that month.

Christmas day fell on a Sunday that year. We had spent the night at Mark and Amy's house rather than at my house, which I thought would be good because it was something different from the norm. I am not sure if it helped. Pam, Steven, and I came home early the next morning to prepare for church. I draw strength from being in our church, but it was still a very painful day. Of all the holidays, Christmas was the most difficult. It is the one time when it was important to have all my family together. But, the one we needed the most, was not there.

I remember sitting in the service and praying that God would help me to lay aside my grief so I could see anew, the Christ of Christmas. Then it came to me, that I did not have to lay aside my grief, nor did God expect me to; I only had to see Him through my grief. And He was indeed there — in every carol that was sung, every prayer that was prayed, and every word that was spoken.

Sunday, January 1, 1995

"Jesus Christ is the same yesterday, and today, and forever."
Hebrews 13:9 (NIV)

"Dear Lord, my world has turned upside down; everything is so uncertain and frightening. I am thankful for your unchanging love."
~Bless Your Heart, Series II, Heartland Samplers, Inc.

The first day of the new year was another difficult day. In years past, I had oftentimes asked myself, "I wonder what the new year is going to hold for us this year?" I suppose it is by God's grace that none of us know what is ahead for each of us. I did feel somewhat fearful of the future; the biggest fear, that of being alone and lonely. Yet, there were so many people who were in the same situation as I that I might possibly help if I had been able to get past my own pain. I really wanted to be used of God in some meaningful way. Perhaps, when this season of grieving was past, and I was able to look to the future, instead of so much to the past, then I felt I would be more useful to others.

SUNDAY, JANUARY 29, 1995

This was a significant day in the life of our family and our church. The Higher Ground Ministry television studios were dedicated and renamed — the Charles R. Skaggs Communication Center. It was dedicated during the Sunday School hour with the church staff, the Higher Ground Ministry staff, and our family present. Pam, Amy, and I were each given a corsage of coral roses; Mark and Steven were given coral boutonnieres. This was significant because they were the same color roses that were used on Charles' casket.

Pastor spoke from the book of Joshua, of the crossing over the river, and Joshua's telling the people to place twelve stones there as a remembrance and reminder of God's faithfulness to His people. The bronze plaque on the wall by the studios was to be a comparable reminder for our church and our family. With a voice filled with emotion, I gave a brief word of appreciation, speaking of Charles' quiet spirit, of his working behind the scenes, and of never expecting any recognition because of his love for this ministry.

After the evening service that day, I was home alone and got out the video tapes of the Silver Anniversary Banquet of the Higher Ground Ministry. Charles was one of the speakers. It was the first time I had seen his face or heard his voice since his death. I listened and caught again, his heart for this ministry, and his willingness to "Do whatever it takes to help this ministry grow." I was also struck by some prophetic words he spoke in his speech. He shared some feelings of anger and frustration he had experienced in the ministry. At the end, he said, "Higher Ground will survive without Charlie Skaggs." These words were spoken four months before his death.

I was one of the soloists at this banquet. One of the songs I sang, spoke of trusting God for our needs, and how He is faithful to provide. Of course, I was thinking in terms of the Television Ministry, but this same theme became the testimony of my own life!

Something that really touched my heart was how Charles openly wept as Janet Dalton sang the song, "Find Us Faithful." This song expressed, that as our loved ones go through our things after we have passed away, that we would be found faithful, and would leave a legacy that would inspire others, particularly our children, to be faithful to God in whatever their calling is in life.

Did he have some sense that he would not be here very long? Perhaps so. But, if our children cannot look back and realize their daddy's selfless devotion and service, they are blind indeed! The footprints he left behind and his work to get out the Gospel, through this medium, have surely helped lead some to believe. Thank you, Lord, for the legacy he left for our family, not just those of us who were there at that time, but also for those who come after him.

When I think of the growth of this ministry, as it is today, with outreach of live broadcasting to neighboring communities, and around the world global viewing of our services through the internet, I am so thankful for a man named Charles Skaggs. He had the vision — he just did not live long enough to see it fulfilled.

Monday, January 30, 1995

On this Monday morning, Pam and I were to drive to Nashville for her interview at Vanderbilt University Hospital to be chosen for 'clinicals' and her year of study to become a medical technologist. We woke up to snow covered roads and school closings all around us.

She came into my room asking what we were going to do. The selections were to be made in two days — she had to be at that interview! I said we were going to pray for God's protection and go! Shortly, I looked into her room. She was crying and said, "Mom, if Dad were here, he would have taken the day off and driven us." He would never have allowed the two of us to start off in bad weather. But, Dad was <u>not</u> here, and we had to go it alone. That was something I was having to learn. Sometimes, I just had to make a decision and go with it. But, God always seemed to place someone in my path to encourage me and to meet specific needs. He must love me a lot to send so many people to help me!

We made it to Nashville and back just fine, with only a few minor 'scares.' The roads were wet but not really slick or icy. I told Pam I had asked God to place His protecting angels before, beside, and behind us; and that is what I envisioned as we drove along — unseen angels, but angels seen through eyes of faith.

Pam did not make it into Vanderbilt that year, but she reapplied and made it the next year. However, it was a great disappointment. I know of nothing she wanted more, other than marrying Doug. Sometimes God's answers are "wait."

Mark and Amy had a great personal disappointment also. They lost a little one. She was not very far along, but it was still a great hurt for them and for the rest of our family.

Saturday, March 25, 1995

And then came Pam and Doug's wedding day.

"May our Lord Jesus Christ himself and God our Father, who loved us and by His grace gave us eternal encouragement and good hope, encourage your hearts and strengthen you in every good deed and word." II Thessalonians 2:16-17 (NIV)

"Thank you, Lord, for this promise of your steadfast love. I am so thankful that no situation I face is too difficult if You are with me. Give me the faith to persevere."
~Bless Your Heart, Series II, Heartland Samplers, Inc.

I looked forward to this day and dreaded it at the same time. We had been so busy getting through all the parties and preparations; yet, the closer the day came, the more anxious I became. This was one occasion I did not know if I could get through without Charles. Sometime during the day, on Friday, before the rehearsal dinner, the realization came to me, that I would make it! And, His incredible peace came into my heart. Later, when I shared this with Pam, she said the same thing had happened to her also, when she slipped on her wedding gown the next day.

With Pam's wedding, as in other occasions, God met specific needs in specific ways. There were anonymous monetary gifts left in my office. There were people participating in the wedding itself, who would not accept an honorarium for their services. And everything about the wedding went so smoothly. God, in His awareness of all things, knew that I needed everything to go smoothly!

When Mark and I rounded the corner to start down the aisle, I took a huge big breath when I saw the single candle burning in the baptistery, placed there in memory of Charles. Mark quietly said, "Mom, it's going to be okay." And it was. When the organ began to play the processional for Pam, and I stood up, I wondered, for a brief moment, if I could turn and watch my two sons walk their sister down the aisle instead of her daddy. But, when I looked at them, they were all three chatting quietly and laughing as they walked! I knew what the boys were doing. They were keeping things light, not only for Pam, but for themselves as well! I recognized again, that God's grace was going to be sufficient for another time in our lives. Even Pastor Randy mentioned the presence of peace in that gathering as he performed the ceremony.

After the reception, they left for their honeymoon, and their new home in Kentucky. That night, I thought my heart would break. It felt as though I were losing Charles all over again. There were many days when I missed Pam almost as much as Charles. But, she was happy and that was the most important thing to me.

Life After Charles

Immediately after the wedding, Steven got involved in baseball. Amy and I drove to Florida to be with him during spring break. I believe he really did need us, although he would never have admitted it. I knew this part of his life was really hard without Charles. But God is good; Steven and I had something to keep us busy for the first part of the summer. I did worry about him; he spoke so little of what he was really feeling. I think I had envisioned this great closeness developing between us after Pam left, but it did not happen at that time. That caused me great pain. I needed so much to feel close to him; I think he needed that too. But, I also had to remember he was at that age when teenage boys are not too communicative anyway, to try to understand, and be there if he needed me.

Steven broke his hand during All-Star season. Of course, that kept him from being able to play. I believe it hurt me more than it did him. He handled it very well in the beginning, but later on, some frustration began showing up in different ways. He went to Beach Camp that year with the youth group. There, he began to acknowledge and deal with some of the anger he was feeling.

As far as friends, both Eleanor and Sandy were very faithful. I spent more time with them that summer than I had in a long time. Many others called for lunch, or invited me out after church, or just called to check on me. The church staff were all so considerate, and the girls who worked with me were wonderful.

My family was good to me, especially my sister, Shirley. She was always ready to listen when I needed to talk. I gained a better understanding of my mother during this time. She expressed more grief at Charles' death than she did for Dad. Or, as one person said, she was hurting because her little girl was hurting.

My brother Neill, spent much time helping with my financial affairs. My brother Glenn, was gone a lot on his job, but he called often to check on me.

There were many times when loneliness threatened to overwhelm me. I often found myself crying when I was at the house alone. But, tears are cleansing, and each morning was a new day. Busyness helped, but at times, nothing I did seemed to make much sense. I did not feel that I had much purpose anymore, that I was just drifting along. I hoped that when I was able to get through the terrible pain that was so much a part of me, then I would be able to see the "new thing" that God wanted to do with my life.

Speaking of a 'new thing,' Jeanne, Pastor Randy's wife, called me to see if I would be one of the conference leaders for the Wonderful Weekend for Women that was coming up in October. I was really surprised; but as soon as I hung up the phone, the question came immediately to my mind, "Lord, are you going to use this to open the door for some 'new thing' in my life?"

One night, a friend told me I needed to let go of Charles, that if I allowed myself to live in the past, I would miss the blessings He had for me in the future. I suppose she was right, but I still felt so tied to Charles, that I was still his wife, and not his widow. How I hated that word! I was so used to being a part of a 'couple,' I certainly did not care for the word 'single.' I was still trying to find out what that meant. I still thought of everything in relation to Charles and what he would do or how he would feel. I was having to learn who I was all over again.

So much of who I had been, was tied to who Charles was — his wife, a deacon's wife, wife of a church staff member, mother of his children, etc. When your main focus for so many years had been wife/mother, it was hard to drop those roles. But, one role was completed. I was no longer a wife.

My covenant with Charles was finished. Scripturally, I was no longer bound by that covenant — but in my heart, I still was. My role as a mother was also changing. Steven would be going away to college in three years, and would not need me so much then. After children become adults, and 'leave the nest,' the role changes to being more friend, than mother. That too, was as it should be.

Our friend and neighbor, Duane Kelly, the one who had suffered a light heart attack in Florida four days before Charles died, had to have a quadruple bypass surgery on Tuesday, May 30th. I went down to Knoxville to be with Sandy and her boys. But, somewhere in our conversation, I began to cry. That certainly was not what she needed, so I apologized and left shortly thereafter. I held it as best I could until I got to the car. Then, the tears flowed freely all the way home. I found myself reliving those days at Ft. Sanders Hospital the past August. The pain seemed as fresh as it did then. But, I can truly say, even today, that I never, in any way, resented the fact that Duane's heart issues turned out so much better than Charles' issues. Sandy has always been a good friend, and I was able to eventually share this with her.

The end of the school year at WEE School rolled around, and with it, the special program called Awards Day. It was always a significant time for the preschoolers and for their parents. It meant their little ones were getting ready to start kindergarten in the fall. It was significant for me that year also. At the end of the program, one of the mothers got up to speak. She spoke of the difficult year I had experienced after losing my husband at the beginning of the school year. The parents had given a memorial gift to the Television Ministry in Charles' memory. I was very touched by this gesture. I spoke briefly, expressing my appreciation. I also shared how working with the children had been so helpful to me. I was so grateful for the job, because for a short time in my day, it took me out of myself. When you work with young children, you have to basically leave your problems at the door. They deserve our full attention. At least, that is what I had always told any new employee who came to work for me. That year, I was really having to learn to 'practice what I preached!'

In June of that year, Steven and I were invited to go along on the Charles R. Skaggs Memorial Mission Trip to Indiana. I was not one for striking out on such a venture without Charles, but we agreed to go. And somewhere along the way, I believe God used this trip to help in my healing process.

We worked in Rockville, Indiana, putting up walls of a small church. At the end of the week, we drove to Clinton, Indiana, to a church that Charles had helped build the previous summer, two months before he died. The pastor of that church met with our group for breakfast before we left. He spoke of Charles and his hard work the year before, and then presented me with a certificate, and a large picture depicting Christ in the clouds with his arms around a man. I envisioned it was Charles being welcomed into heaven.

Back home that Sunday night, a report of the trip was given to the church. Then, Steven and I were called down to the front. We were given a presentation and Steven was highly praised for all the hard work he had done. I had already told him how proud his dad would have been. I shared some of my feelings about the trip, about praying to have a servant heart like Charles, and thanked all the encouragers on the trip. I was actually able to speak without crying! I could feel God's healing was at work.

Trading cars was an eye-opening experience. Charles had always done the 'wheeling and dealing' when a car was being purchased. But, I took Steven with me, and we ended up with a fairly good deal.

Several days later I realized I still did not have a peace about it. As I sat thinking about it one afternoon, I got a picture in my mind of Charles' face, and he was smiling at me. It was as if he were saying, "You did good, Honey." From then on, I felt complete peace.

Learning To Cope

So many things changed in my life. Even my so-called 'social life' was so very different. People who have couples events do not usually invite a single woman. We used to go to deacons and wives dinners, Brotherhood and wives dinners, and Sunday school functions as a couple. I continue to be invited to some things; however, I often felt uncomfortable and out of place. I did go out occasionally with some female friends, but it was just not the same. But then, not much in my life was the same anyway.

Things were different at church also. I just could not seem to find my 'place' in the sanctuary. I sat in many different areas, but nothing felt right to me. I almost felt like a visitor at times, and usually ended up sitting in the balcony simply because Mark was there operating the soundboard, a position Charles had held for so many years. I suppose nothing felt right because my 'place' was in the choir loft, where it had been since I was a teenager; but music touches my heart and emotions like nothing else, and tears were still very close to the surface. Also, the first thing I would do upon entering the choir loft, was to look up at the sound booth and make eye contact with Charles. I hoped that someday I would be able to return to the choir and sing again.

In regard to the emotion, this grieving can really 'blindside' you at times. You go along thinking you are doing so well. Then, something happens — a particular memory suddenly pops in your mind; perhaps you have a dream; you might hear a certain song; you might hear a voice that sounds like his; or you recall some silly thing he used to say — and immediately you are swept down into the abyss of sorrow again. But thankfully, as time went by, those times became fewer and farther apart. I am grateful the memories I have were great ones. As the years have passed, I am able to look back on those memories with tenderness and laughter, and they do not carry such a weight of pain anymore.

I wrote earlier about God's preparation. I remember when Pastor Randy came to our church, two years before Charles died. He preached often about the trials and storms of life. I remember one thing that helped me tremendously. He said that God did not promise we would be free from storms, but that He would walk with us through those storms. I have really clung to that promise. Charles and I had discussed the fact that the pastor was preaching so much on this subject. We decided there must have been a lot of hurting people in our church at that time.

Now, in looking back, I believe God was preparing me for this time in my life. Also, Charles taught Steven how to do many little things around the house, such as changing fuses, things I do not recall his having taught Mark when he was younger and still at home. This probably seems coincidental or insignificant to some, but God uses even the small things to help us.

I often struggled with fear. I remember that right after Charles died, I was hesitant to go out into the neighborhood to walk, as I was accustomed to doing. He always sat on the front porch and waited for me to return. If I was not back within 30 minutes, he would get in the car and come looking for me. Another fear was staying by myself at night. Charles did not work in jobs that required his being out of town at night. This was something else I had to overcome. I was fearful of driving in big cities. Charles always did the driving, so I did not have any experience. This too, I had to learn to do.

Praise and Thanksgiving

Through all of this first year, I began to feel grateful for many things, one of which was, that I was able to keep my same job, that our needs were met, sometimes in miraculous ways, and I did not have to seek full-time employment. The world looks for youth and beauty, along with skills. At the time of Charles' death, I was 48 years old, so youth was out; I never had much beauty to begin with; and what skills I once had, were obsolete, with so much new computer skill being required. Thus, the thought of going out into the world, away from the shelter of my church job was really frightening to me. I suppose I had been too protected from the world being a stay-at-home mom with a part-time job.

I was also grateful that I did not have to sell our home. In every room, I could see Charles' handiwork. We never called a repairman — Charles did everything from light maintenance, to major remodeling, to putting a roof on the house. I started realizing how expensive repair work could be!

Of course, other than my Heavenly Father, my highest gratitude went to my precious children, and the rest of my family, for their constant expressions of love and support. How I pity those who have no children to share such a burden! Charles' death bonded our family together as nothing else could have done.

I had to practice praise many times when I did not feel like praising. But then, God does not say we are to praise Him just when we feel like it, does He? Esther Walker, a former pastor's wife, often talked about praise, using scripture referencing that He inhabits the praise of His people. I certainly needed His habitation in my life! I tried to make a practice of finding something positive whenever I felt myself getting 'down.' Sometimes, God had to 'nudge' me when I was feeling particularly low.

My feelings of self-worth really took a 'beating' at times. I found this can happen when you no longer feel fulfilled or complete. Charles was my chief protector, my friend, my lover, my best critic, my best supporter. So many dreams would now go unfulfilled and unrealized. There were many things we wanted to do together after Steven went away to college, things we never had the time or resources to do — a cruise to the Caribbean, a trip in autumn to New England, a screened-in porch where we would wile away the evening hours on a summer night. I would be reading a book, and he would be — well, what else — taking a nap! Whatever the reason, God's timing is never wrong, no matter how much we may question. I just had to keep trusting in that!

The peace He gave me was nothing short of miraculous. And yet, I should not have been surprised — He promised it in His Word! He proved to be everything He had promised to be; and even though the pain was very deep, so was the peace. I suppose that was why I did not experience the anger toward God, that's always listed in grief books as one of the stages of grief. At the time of this original writing, a year had not yet passed, so I knew it was still a possibility. My father had only been a Christian for three months when he died. My sister once asked me how I was able to deal so well with his death. My response was, that I was so grateful that I knew where he was. This time; however, I had only myself and God in those very darkest hours, and in the deepest recesses of my heart and spirit. And again, He came through for me — His grace is sufficient.

I spoke of Charles often (to anyone who would listen!). I probably bored people with it. I guess I sometimes forgot that even though the thoughts of his passing were constantly uppermost in my mind, others had passed on beyond it. It did help to speak of him, if nothing else, that it made him seem that he was still here, when I mentioned something he said or did, as though it were yesterday.

One of the positive things I gained from this experience was that I no longer fear death. Many times, we can be fearful of that of which we have no personal knowledge, other than what we read in Scripture. But now, because of the wonderful dying grace, and the peace I saw in Charles, I can look to my own death without fear.

One thing my friend Nancy Eversole told me after her husband passed away, was that we do not remember any of the bad things. This was true. Charles and I did not have a perfect life, although it was a good life. But we do tend to remember only the very best of the person who dies. That was, and still is true of my remembrances of Charles. I loved him dearly, but I knew he was not perfect, nor was I. Somehow, anything less than good, I seemed to have forgotten, or at least, I pushed it back into the farthest corners of my mind.

I often wondered why God gave Charles the position at our church that he loved so much and then took him away so soon. We had prayed about it and both believed it was where God wanted him to be. Charles told a friend right after he started work there that he felt as if he had come home. I also wondered why the heart attack happened there rather than the job he had just left. I did not have the answers to these questions, other than it was a part of God's provision for Steven and me. There were death benefits through the church I would not have received otherwise. God is good!

REFLECTIONS

That first year went by. I had passed through some deep waters, but they did not 'sweep over me.' Many times, I wondered if I would ever 'make it to shore.' In fact, I was still struggling in my journey of healing. Some days, it was two steps forward and three steps back. But, I just kept picking myself up and starting over again, seeking God's help as I went.

I had always believed if I could just make it through that first year, I would be okay. I guess I thought something magical was going to happen — but, it did not. It still hurt just as much as it did a year earlier when Charles died. Yet, I was learning to deal with it a little better each day. God is a faithful God, and I knew that He was working to take all the broken pieces of my life and put them back together again. How I longed for that day — when I could feel like a whole person again!

God was teaching me all along grief's journey. One thing I learned was, that our security does not lie in the things of this life — not even in our mate — only in God, and our hope of heaven. "When God is all you have, then you find He is all you need." I was very dependent on Charles in many areas of my life. His death forced me to learn a new dependence on God alone. That is where my true dependence should have been all along. There were times that year when I did not always 'feel' God's presence, yet, I knew He was still there, just a prayer's breath away. I also learned I had to make a new life for myself, one that did not revolve solely around my children and family. They had their own lives to live, and I was really trying not to hang onto them too selfishly. I determined to be content to be just a small part of their lives.

Having said all that, I often found myself feeling very lonely. Sometimes, being busy helped; at other times, I just had to give in to the pain, and allow it to run its course. I did not know the plans God had for my life, but I had reached the point of asking Him, as the Apostle had asked of God, that He help me to be content in whatever circumstance I found myself; whether I was to live the rest of my life alone, or whether He might choose to send someone else to share my life.

The question, 'why,' was still unanswered, but I did accept it, by faith.

God is sovereign and was under no obligation to explain anything to me. I just had to believe that:

> "God is too good to be unkind;
> God is too wise to be mistaken;
> When you cannot trace His hand,
> You can always trust His heart."
> ~Babbie Mason

THE TRANSITION

The following year and a half was spent working, being with family and friends, renewing my involvement with different church ministries, and learning how to live without Charles. I was still very lonely; yet, I seemed to have a sense of anticipation that God had something else planned for my life.

Someone once suggested that I publish the 'Part One – Charles Skaggs' portion of this book. For some reason, I never felt the time was right. Little did I know that I was going to have another whole lifetime (although it was a short one), about which to write!

The following pages detail my life with Louie Vesser, from the beginning of our courtship through his death, and how God would again, be my 'refuge and strength.'

Louie and Peggy Vesser
July 18, 1998

Part Two

Louie Vesser

"Some people come into our lives and quickly go. Some people move our souls to dance. They awaken us to a new understanding with the passing whisper of their wisdom. Some people make this life more beautiful to gaze upon. They stay in our lives for a while, leave footprints on our hearts, and we are never ever the same."

~Flavia Weedn

"You turned my wailing into dancing; you removed my sackcloth and clothed me with joy, that my heart may sing your praises and not be silent. Lord my God, I will praise you forever." Psalm 30: 11-12 (NIV)

Charles had been gone almost 2 ½ years. In 1996, during the Christmas holidays, I had reached 'rock bottom' in my spirit. I was so depressed and lonely I did not think I could face another year. Even my children were not able to get me out of my 'doldrums,' as they usually were able to do.

On New Year's Eve, my friend, Janet Dalton, invited me to attend a party of another friend in Sevierville. I really felt strange going to a 'singles' party, although there were couples there, as well as single people. I still found it difficult to think of myself as 'single.'

We ate dinner, visited, and played games. I mostly sat on the sidelines feeling uncomfortable. I saw Louie Vesser there. Of course, he was laughing and making jokes. I knew who he was from having seen him around church, but I had never spoken with him, nor did I know much about him. On the way home, Janet, who also happened to be a good friend of Louie's, kept talking about him, and seemed to be 'feeling me out' to see if I were interested in dating him. At that time, I was not interested.

Later on in January, Louie and I were attending a birthday party for our mutual friend Clay Krummel. Louie had written a special poem about Clay, and I remember thinking it was quite good. Again, different people, including Janet, were trying to get us together. Nothing happened; however, although I did notice several times when I looked his way, Louie was looking at me. Later on, after we did begin dating, he told me at that time, he was afraid I was not yet ready to begin dating (Janet had been working on him, too!).

Sometime around the middle of January, I was so depressed that one night I fell to my knees beside my bed and prayed (as I had done once before), that God would once again help me to be content, whether alone, or with someone who might be in my future. I think I had to go through complete brokenness, and having a willingness to accept His will, no matter what it was, before God could work out His plan for my life (and Louie's)!

It was February 4, 1997. I was at home in my den. Steven was in his room doing homework when the phone rang. When I picked it up and answered, it was Louie Vesser. He asked if I would have dinner with him the following Friday evening. And, wonder of wonders, I heard myself saying, "Yes, I would love to have dinner with you." I was so excited, and a little apprehensive. After all, I had not had a date in many years, since Charles and I were in high school. What would I wear? What would I talk about? Would he find me boring? All these questions and many more kept flowing through my head.

Friday night rolled around and Louie picked me up right on time. We drove to the Little Dutch Restaurant, a popular Friday night place to eat. We were right out in the middle of the restaurant. While there, some of his friends from Jefferson County, where he lived and worked, walked by and did double takes when they saw us. After eating, we went to the basketball game between Jefferson County, where Louie was a vice-principal, and West High School in Morristown, where his son Justin played. There, we saw many shocked faces from other people from our church. Louie said later, that there were people in two counties talking about us that night.

It was a very good evening, filled with conversation and laughter. Upon arriving home, he stated he had a really good time, and would I consider doing this again sometime. I also had a good time and agreed to go out with him again. My friend, Carolyn Barclay, said that if he called me back within two weeks for another date, he was interested. Guess what — I got a call from him on Sunday night, three nights later, asking for another date for the next week. He was definitely interested!

From then on, my life was never the same! Louie Vesser roared into my life, bringing robust laughter — no, downright hilarity at times, and a whole new world of new restaurants, plays, new friends, travel, and a relationship of sharing, caring, and finding ways to please me that made me the envy of all my friends, both married and single! There were constant surprises. I only had to mention wanting to go somewhere or do something special, and he made it his mission to see that it happened. One of my friends laughingly said once, that Louie should hold a seminar for husbands on "How to Treat Your Mate."

His reason for finally calling me was to be found in Scripture. He had a devotional calendar on his desk at school. On the particular day he called, it was turned to James 1:27, the one stating "true and undefiled religion is taking care of the widows and orphans." This was his 'sign from heaven' that he was to call and ask me out on a date!

One of the things that drew me to Louie was his ability to listen. I was basically a shy person and was really nervous on our first date. But, he had such a wonderful ability to draw people out and engage them in conversation. I was no exception. He put me at ease right away. He was also very considerate of my feelings for Charles. We spoke of him sometimes. He told me he had nothing but admiration and respect for Charles. Once, about a year after we were married, I was asked to speak at our church's Television Ministry Banquet. Louie attended with me and listened intently as I spoke in glowing terms of my former husband's hard work and vision for the ministry. Louie even complimented me profusely on the speech I had given. How many men would have been so generous about a wife's former husband? Only Louie Vesser!

On our third date, we were at a play at the Cumberland County Playhouse. It involved the death of the husband and father of the family. I was crying softly beside Louie. He quietly reached for his handkerchief, handed it to me, and briefly put his hand over mine. It was such a small gesture of kindness, but it began showing me the sensitivity and heart of this man. I think that was when I began to fall in love again. The real miracle was, that this intelligent, witty, and gifted man was also falling in love with me!

Louie's generous spirit and sensitivity were most evident in how he dealt with my children. My older two were grown and married; Steven was a junior in high school by this time. He was still struggling with grief over losing his father, and he had difficulty seeing his mother with another man. Louie did not push himself on Steven, nor on the other two. Pam and Doug were the first ones to really accept him. She once said, "Mom, how could we not accept him when we could see how happy he had made you?" The boys were a little slower coming around (which is normal for boys, I think, where their mother is concerned), but they did eventually accept him also. My extended family accepted him as well. In fact, we went on several excursions with my sister, Shirley, and her husband, Buddy, and had a wonderful time with them.

We had a true whirlwind courtship and a genuine love affair with each other. I believe part of this was due to the timing. We were both alone and lonely, and our children were all grown up by this time. We had plenty of time to devote to each other and time to build a relationship.

He was a very romantic man, constantly writing me notes, and sending cards that told of his love for me. He called my workplace often, and sent flowers there and to my home. The basis of our relationship was our faith in God and our belief that He was the one who had brought us together. Our special verse was Jeremiah 29:11 NASB. "For I know the plans I have for you, declares the Lord, plans for welfare, and not for calamity, to give you a future and a hope."

Sometime into the relationship, Louie asked me to go to meet his family at his mother's house. Betty (or Sadie, as Louie called her) had prepared a wonderful meal. I was never so nervous in my life as I was that night! I felt like a teenager on a first date! But, Sadie, Charlie, Louie's brother; his wife, Cheryl; and their son, Chaz, quickly made me feel right at home, and the evening went quite well.

In June of that year, Louie convinced me to take a trip to Australia with him and a group from the high school. Talk about a real stretch! I had only been on an airplane twice in my life, and to get on a plane, and go halfway around the world with strangers, and with a man I had only known a few months, was really pushing it! Louie was very persuasive; however, and my children encouraged me to go. So, I went! It was a wonderful experience that I will always remember, and it gave us a chance to get to know each other in different circumstances than our usual ones here at home. Also, his sons, Josh and Justin, went on the trip; and I got to know them a little better.

My family was waiting at the airport to take me home when we arrived back in Knoxville. Louie and I said our goodbyes. We agreed he would not contact me for a few days to allow us to recover from the jet lag he knew we would have. At about 1:00 p.m. the next day, the phone rang. Guess who? He said we had just spent twelve days together and he could not stand not hearing my voice that day. We talked briefly, then made a date for the next night. So much for jet lag!

Our whole courtship was a whirlwind of activity, adventures, and surprises. It could be as simple as a picnic and Johnny Mathis music on a hillside in Cade's Cove, or as grand as a romantic dinner in a restaurant atop the largest hotel in Australia. We talked constantly on every date and in every phone call. We never seemed to run out of things to discuss, but that was Louie. There was always conversation when he was around. The times we did happen to be quiet, were comfortable and easy, when we both knew conversation was not necessary.

In December of 1997, Louie took me to the Knoxville Symphony Christmas Concert. After returning home, he suggested we go for a ride to look at Christmas lights. I asked Steven to go along, but he declined. We got back into Louie's truck, but he did not start the engine. He just sat there, shaking. I thought he was cold, but when he began to speak, I realized it was nerves! This man, who could go before thousands, speak and control a crowd, was visibly shaking from nerves! That was the night we became engaged. As he was placing the diamond solitaire on my finger, he said he wanted to take care of me for the rest of his life — and he did, for the rest of his short life. Steven did not accompany us because he was aware of what was taking place. It seems Louie had spoken to my children to make sure it was okay to ask me to marry him, or, in the old fashioned sense, to 'ask for my hand in marriage.'

That same weekend was our church's presentation of the Living Christmas Tree. I learned that two other women in our choir had gotten engaged the same weekend as Louie and I. The three of us women were in the top-most three positions of the Tree. The pastor told the congregation, that if there were any unmarried women out there looking for a husband, just come and sing in the top of the Living Christmas Tree!

We bought a lot in the Patriot Hills subdivision in Jefferson City in February and began construction on our house. My birthday was in

March. Louie called me that day to say we were going to do something different and special that year. As it turned out, he had cooked a complete meal and had his son, Justin, carry it out to our lot where the house was being built. When we arrived, Justin was gone. A card table was set up on the back part of the lot with a tablecloth, a candle, flowers, and "*Unforgettable*" playing on a tape player. We ate and danced on the lot overlooking the huge hole that was to be our basement. What a romantic and innovative guy I was marrying!

We were married by Danny Georges in our church parlor on July 18th, 1998, with just our two families present. All of our children stood up with us. It was the beginning of a love affair that continued until the day he died. We left for our honeymoon in the Cayman Islands. When we returned, the house was not yet completed, so we spent a couple of days at Pam and Doug's house until it was at the point we could move in.

Louie loved his sons very much; but, they were very busy, as were we. We did not get to spend as much time with them as we would have liked. Louie embraced my children and family and loved them as his own. Our home became a gathering place for many get-togethers, particularly on the holidays. Between our two families, we could have as many as 20 or more people for a meal on Thanksgiving or Christmas. Louie loved opening our home to others and having a great time together with family or friends.

Our family increased in 1999; with another daughter-in-law, Morgan; and two grandchildren, Tyler and Isabella, born 2 1/2 months apart, whom Louie dubbed, the "Prince and Princess." You would have thought we were the only two people in the world who had ever become grandparents, "Grandmom and Pop." In 2002; we added Shelton and Emily, born two weeks apart; and in 2003, Wil came along. Then, in 2004, little Molly was born. Louie could not have been more proud of these children had they been his blood grandchildren. He loved each of them the same. In June of 2002; we also added another daughter-in-law, Amy, who married Justin. With the increase of so many more people added to our family, our lives became even more busy.

In April of 2001, another storm was brewing on my horizon. My mother was diagnosed with Alzheimer's disease. This was right after her 83rd birthday. We had hosted a birthday dinner in our home with my brothers, sister, and spouses. I was so glad we had gotten them all together as a family to honor her.

After the diagnosis, my sister and brothers, and I began the process of looking after her. Thankfully, she was able to remain in her home until she died that same year of a massive stroke, two days after Christmas. Again, God's grace was in action. I believe our family was spared all the hard things that come to Alzheimer patients and to their families and caregivers.

It was particularly hard losing my mother. It seemed that with Dad's death, and now hers, my childhood went with her, along with memories that only she could recall about our family. And we had just lost Shirley's' son, David, in October of that same year. This was an especially difficult time for our family. In August of 2004; my brother Glenn's wife, Jackie, passed away suddenly in their home. Our extended family was really changing.

Overall, our lives were busy and happy. Louie was a man of much vision and was instrumental in starting many new programs at the high school, and served on many boards and committees in our community. He had friends wherever he went. He had a love for people and a zest for life that I have not seen in many people. Upon meeting new people, he quickly put them at ease. He had an extremely quick wit, a creative mind, and a special kind of wisdom that made him very good at his job working with teenagers. One of his favorite sayings was, "Life is made up of challenges, not problems." That is how he looked at life. His 'vitamin' of life was laughter. He had an infectious laugh that started at the top of his head and went all the way down to his toes.

Outside of his family, his greatest contributions were made as assistant principal of the local high school. He was well-liked by students and faculty alike. He was a friend and mentor to both students and teachers. His door was always open to either group. He had a genuine concern for the students, not only for their education, but for their personal well-being also.

DECEMBER, 2004

In December of 2004, Louie was nominated for, and selected as, the Assistant Principal of the Year for the state of Tennessee. What a wonderful honor and so well-deserved! He was to be recognized at a seminar in San Francisco in late February, 2005, and we made our plans to go. God's timing was a work of grace in this event also.

Another storm had been brewing since December, however. Louie's health had been deteriorating. We both knew it, although we did not speak of it. He had been a diabetic for 15 years, and now he was beginning to show signs of some of the complications of the disease. He had already fallen several times, beginning at the start of the school year in August. He broke his arm but recovered and was soon back with his usual busy schedule.

In late December, after some tests, one of his doctors told him he was a "train wreck waiting to happen." That certainly was not what we wanted to hear, but it was not a real surprise. That was a dark day for us.

We went ahead with the San Francisco trip, along with our friends; Dale and Mandy Schneitman; and two other couples from Maryville. We had a marvelous trip with much fun, laughter, and sightseeing. Louie's sense of humor kept us laughing everywhere we went.

It was on this trip that I really began to realize just how much Louie's strength and stamina were beginning to wane. But, he was a proud man and he would not allow others to see he was having difficulty. I am sure Dale was aware since he worked with him every day at school.

Once however; on our way to Big Sur, we made a stop by the roadside, overlooking the bluffs that went down to the ocean. Louie remained in the van with the side door open. I, along with the others, walked over to the edge to look out over the ocean. When I got close to the edge, Louie called out for me to come back. When I did, he said, "P. J., please don't go back over there again; I need you too much." That remark really surprised me. I always felt it was I who needed him.

When we returned home, Louie got back into his same demanding schedule, pushing himself to finish plans for all the activities coming up at the end of the school year. In my head, I knew he was getting weaker; but in my heart, I did not want to admit it. There were days he would come through the door, at the end of his day, and I honestly, did not know if he would make it to his chair. But, he had an amazing ability to recover after a bit of rest and a good meal.

I always seemed to have a feeling that something ominous was just around the corner. I watched him closely, all the time, hoping that he did not notice. Months later, others at the school told me of incidents that were happening there that caused them to watch also.

We were scheduled to fly to Washington, D.C. on Thursday, April 7th, for the formal reception and awards banquet for the Assistant Principal of the Year. The previous Friday, Louie had gone to a local shop to be fitted for a tuxedo for the banquet. Sometime in the afternoon, I got a call from the shop owner, stating that Louie had fallen. My heart began racing as I could hear the ambulance siren in the background. The shop owner assured me Louie was okay; however, since he had hit his head in the fall, he was being taken to the hospital to be checked. As it turned out, he was fine, except for being very sore.

This was also the evening of the funeral for my nephew Terry. Terry, was my brother Neill's son. Louie was unable to attend, but he insisted on going to the graveside service the next morning. He had to use a cane, but he still needed assistance from me. This was certainly an 'eye-opener' for many of my family who had not seen him in some time, to see the condition he was in.

Over the weekend, he began saying he did not think we should go on the Washington trip. By Monday, he was feeling better, and decided we would go after all. We left on a Thursday morning. At the airport, he experienced another fall trying to get his suitcase up over the curb. Two men came and helped me get him up. From then on, both in Knoxville, and in Washington, he rode in wheelchairs through the airports.

When we arrived at our hotel in Washington, I knew he was really tired, so I suggested we just rest for a bit; but, he insisted on going out sightseeing. I tried to discourage him, but he said something I will always remember. "We may never get back to Washington again." Did he have some sense of what was on the horizon for us? Perhaps so. We rode in cabs wherever we went, and he struggled to get his legs lifted up and into the vehicles. As usual; however, he pushed himself and we made it through the rest of our stay there without further incident.

At the banquet, he was not his usual 'chatty' self. I, on the other hand, the shy, quieter one, was the more talkative one in this instance. Later, he said he was proud of me for conversing with everyone at our table. When the time came for him to receive his recognition, I realized he would not be able to get up on the platform. He had already worked it out with the banquet planner. When his name was called, the men giving out the recognitions left the platform and came down on the floor level to him. This was a very considerate gesture on their part.

I was beginning to realize just how serious the neuropathy was in his feet and that it was getting much worse. This was the reason for the many falls he was having. His feet were so numb, they were unable to move fast enough to catch him when he got over-balanced. Louie was a large man; and when he fell, he went down hard. Also, his vision had gotten much worse. He had already had several eye surgeries the previous summer. He still drove himself to school, which was only five minutes away, and sometimes into town. I did most of the driving at this point, especially at night.

On Tuesday night, May 3rd, the high school held their first Senior Celebration at the local college instead of the high school. Louie had planned it down to the last detail. I was aware that he was not feeling well. As I sat with Mandy in the stands, and watched him move around, I could not help but be concerned. There were no handrails up to the platform where he was to speak.

I mentioned this to Mandy, whose husband was the principal, and she went to speak with him about it. Dale stated that he and the other principals were already aware of the problem. He assured her that they had it covered.

He was helped up to the platform. But, when his time came to speak, he was hardly able to get up out of his chair. In fact, two of the men practically lifted him up. When he spoke, he was literally stumbling over his words. I was stunned. I had never heard him read as he did that evening. This was a man who was an English major, one who had spoken for functions all his life! Words were his forte. I sat there, with tears in my eyes, as I observed him. I realized why he had asked me to drive that night. Usually, he drove himself and I would come later. I was beginning to feel that the "train wreck" was imminent.

Thursday, May 5th, 2005

Then came Thursday evening, May 5th, 2005, the day when the downward spiral began. He had come in from school that afternoon. We were discussing the events of the day. For the first time, in several weeks, he seemed more like his old self than he had in a long time.

I had a workshop to attend in Morristown, so he was going to drive me, and we would get something to eat on the way. I tried to persuade him to stay home and rest and let me drive myself, but he insisted. Later, after returning home, we watched a little television. He said he had walked in the mall while I attended the workshop. Actually, I found out later, he went shopping for a late birthday present for me. His mother had been in the hospital on my birthday, and we had not celebrated, as was our usual custom.

Around 10:00 p.m., Louie got up to go to bed. We were standing by the snack bar in the kitchen. He bent over to kiss me goodnight. When he raised up, he lost his balance, fell back against the bar, hitting his head, and on down to the floor. We knew immediately that something was broken. I called 911, and Dale and Mandy. They lived up the street from us and arrived at our house before the ambulance.

He was taken to the hospital and was told he had a broken hip. Surgery was scheduled for the next morning, and I prepared to spend the night. Steven came and stayed until around 2:00 a.m. The surgery was scheduled for 11:00 a.m. the next day. He came through the surgery fine; but by Monday, when the therapist started trying to get him out of bed and into a chair, he found that Louie did not have enough arm strength to push himself up off the bed. The therapist continued working with him, but finally realized Louie needed more than he could do. By the end of the week, it was decided, he would go to the Patricia Neal Rehabilitation Center at Ft. Sanders Hospital in Knoxville. He was moved on Friday afternoon by ambulance.

In our minds, we thought he would have a couple of weeks of therapy, and then he would be home. Little did we know, what the upcoming weeks had in store for us! I believe God, in His wisdom, knows we could not handle the future if we knew what it would bring to us.

Louie endured so much! Most of the time, he endured with grace, but there were times when depression and even anger took over. I am sure, with all he went through, many people would have experienced the same emotions. It was at these particular times, when he was so emotionally depleted, that he closed himself off to me, and to everyone else. This was the same man who talked nonstop with me about everything! So much was happening with his body; so many treatments were given, and medications administered, that they oftentimes seemed to work against each other.

After a week in the Rehabilitation Center, he was moved to the acute floor for staph infection in the blood stream. He was given very powerful antibiotics and pretty much quarantined during that period. He was losing blood and given several units of blood, but they were unable to determine the cause of the blood loss. Of course, this involved more tests. At this time, he had reached the point of being unable to move his legs, as the neuropathy was rapidly making its way up his legs, and into the trunk of his body. This meant being put into a lift and placed into a wheelchair. I knew, without a word from Louie, how degrading this was for him.

After a week on the acute floor, he was moved back to the Rehabilitation Center, into the Neurological Unit, rather than the Orthopedic Unit, because of the loss of muscle strength and the different type of therapy he needed. He was measured for a motorized wheelchair and there was discussion of purchasing a handicap van. It was then, that I really began to realize just how serious things were. Also during this time, he began to have significant swelling in his arms, legs, and in his midsection. More tests were performed. It was determined, his kidneys were losing some of their function. I felt as if a huge, dark cloud had settled upon us.

Then a new doctor, a neurologist, came to see us. He believed Louie's neuropathy was not due just to the diabetic neuropathy, but that he had an immune disease, the name being, Immune Mediated Neuropathy. There was treatment for it; however, the drawback was, that it could adversely affect his kidneys, which were already in trouble. Of course, to get a definitive diagnosis, a spinal tap and nerve biopsy had to be done.

For the first time, we were somewhat hopeful; after all, his kidneys were constantly being monitored! We even discussed that perhaps this was the reason for the broken hip. We might never have known about the immune disease had we not been there for the broken hip. We wanted so badly to have some good news. We rationalized and deluded ourselves into thinking things were better than they actually were.

There were more frustrating days of therapy, with Louie getting more and more agitated. Then came the weekend when he became delirious. Fluid was building in his body and his kidneys were not filtering properly. By Monday morning, his condition had worsened considerably. His breathing was very difficult. He had so much fluid, that when he was rolled over to change his bed, the fluid pressed against his lungs. His breathing would drop to 40 or 50%. He was moved to the ICU that morning and I 'set up camp' in the waiting room. Thankfully, I was not alone that first night. My sons; Steven and Mark; Louie's son's, Josh and Justin; his Mother, Sadie; and his brother, Charlie, stayed with me. None of us slept, but at least I had someone with me.

The next day, Louie was taken down to have a CAT scan to determine if the fluid was in his lungs or just within the chest wall. I decided I had time to hurry home, get some clothes, and get back. Steven drove me. As we were walking in the door, the phone was ringing. It was Sadie, calling to say Louie had stopped breathing during the procedure and they were considering putting him on a ventilator. Steven and I rushed right back. I was praying all the way. A ventilator is such a final step, in many cases. When we arrived, thankfully, he had been put on a C-Pap machine instead. God's grace continued to amaze me!

That night, Louie began asking for different family members to come into the room so he could talk with them. He was preparing to die, but God was not ready for him yet! There was a continuous parade of people that night and into the next day through the ICU! I am surprised they did not throw us all out!

Louie told each one what they had meant to him, and basically told them goodbye, without actually saying it. He talked with everyone except me. Some days later, I asked why he did not have any special words for me. I will always remember what he said. "It's like this, P. J., you take your dearest treasure and hold it close to your heart for as long as you can." He was not yet ready to tell me goodbye; that was to come later.

Can you imagine, Reader, what I was feeling? I had already said goodbye to one husband in this very hospital! My mind and emotions were on a roller coaster, constantly. There was fear and anxiety, compassion for what Louie was experiencing, and such a strong sense of dread that I was going to lose him.

I remember early on, when he first went to the rehabilitation unit, I went home to stay one night. I walked into our home and sat down in his favorite chair. I began to weep, and did so for probably an hour, until I could weep no more. I knew, even then, our lives were never going to be the same, even if he did recover enough to come home. My main prayer during this time was for strength for both of us. I also prayed he would not give up. I suppose I was afraid to pray for God's will, because it might not be what I could handle at that time. Yet, even in the midst of the 'roller coaster,' there was a calmness that was keeping me together when I needed to be together — for Louie's sake, and my own. That had to be another product of God's grace working in our lives.

We definitely were in the midst of another storm, one that kept building in intensity. It was not just Louie who was affected, but all the people who cared about him. His mother, Sadie, was recovering from major surgery herself, but she came almost every day to sit with Louie so I could get out of the room for an hour or two. Those walls can quickly close in on you when you are spending all of your time in a hospital room!

Different family members were in and out for short periods of time. Josh and Justin came in. Mark sat with me after work, several times. Amy brought Tyler by to see "Pop." It was amazing how Louie could be really low, but he always managed to bring himself up when Tyler was there. Steven and Morgan came in often. Morgan was the one who could really get Louie to laugh and sound like his old self again. Many co-workers and friends from the high school came, and some of my female friends would come and sit or just spend time with me for brief periods. There were times when I had to discourage visits when Louie was not himself.

And then, there was Janet Dalton. She was a friend of many years, to both of us. She was also the one who was probably most instrumental in getting Louie and me together. I remember one day she came in when

Pam was there. The therapist had been in and wanted Louie to do some exercises (which he did not want to do). The three of us stood around his bed and began doing the exercises, to show him how, with a lot of foolishness in between. We were all laughing our heads off when the nurse came into the room; but, he did the exercises — and we along with him! It was wonderful to hear that laugh of his again!

Mike Hooker, who was Louie's college roommate from Carson Newman College, came and spent many days with us. He was a doctor himself, although disabled and not working. He was able to interpret the mountain of information we received and also helped in coordinating the many doctors we had. Mike stayed with Louie some nights, which afforded me the opportunity to go to Sadie's house occasionally to sleep in a real bed! I did not leave Knoxville again after Louie came out of the ICU. I either stayed at the hospital, or went to Sadie's house, which was only ten minutes away.

After a week in ICU, Louie was moved to the Critical Care Unit (CCU) for a week, then on to his final place, the Nephrology Unit. His kidneys were showing signs of real trouble. Dialysis was discussed as a possible treatment, should it come to that; however, it was also relayed to me, by his kidney doctors, they were not sure his body could withstand this treatment. At any rate, Louie was adamant that he would not undergo dialysis.

TUESDAY, JULY 5TH, 2005

Louie's 54th birthday was Tuesday, July 5th. Pam cooked a complete meal of his favorite things and carried it into his room, along with Doug, the girls, and Steven and Morgan. We all celebrated his birthday with much fun and laughter until he got really tired. They all packed up and left. It was so good to see him eat. He was eating virtually nothing up to this time. I do not know if all the mediation took away his appetite, or he just did not care for the hospital food. Sometimes, I would go to a restaurant and pick up a small steak and salad, which we would share. Occasionally, he would drink the Boost drink, just to give himself some nourishment. But, he did not like to do even that.

More days passed and more of the constant emotional upheaval. It seemed that every time we got some good news, bad news was soon to follow. One day, he was taken to surgery to insert a filter in a vein to prevent blood clots from getting to his heart or lungs. Again, there was so much fluid around his lungs that he almost stopped breathing when he was moved to the surgery table. So, that procedure was not done, which left him at great risk. All the fluid build-up was taking place in spite of the massive doses of diuretics he was receiving. My medical knowledge was minimal, so I did not realize, until later on, that the fluid build-up was most likely an indication of organs shutting down.

Later on that day, the pulmonary doctor came into the room and basically said there was nothing else to be done for Louie. So, Louie promptly asked if he could go home with Hospice. Obviously, it was not a new idea, but something he had been thinking about during all those quiet times he had.

I was dumbfounded, to say the least. So was each person in the room. I sat back in my chair, so taken aback, I could hardly comprehend the discussion between Louie and the doctor. Mike looked completely stunned. Sadie left the room in tears. Although I was not aware of it, Mark and Pam were out in the hallway. Sadie sent Pam in to be with me. Once again, as in many past times, God knew just what I needed, and it was the comfort Pam and Mark gave me, just by being there.

Pam and I stood by Louie's bed as he pleaded with me to please take him home. Finally, I agreed — what else could I do?! When I did agree, it was as though a huge weight had been lifted from his shoulders. The only problem was, that the weight had now shifted and came to rest on my shoulders. All of Louie's adult life, he was in positions of authority and being in charge. I understood he no longer felt he was in control of his own life. This decision, to go home with Hospice, was his way of getting back some of that control.

The next day, one of his doctors tried to get him to change his mind and to allow them to proceed with the treatments that were scheduled. But, he was determined he was going home to die, and he made sure all his doctors understood he wanted to be out of the hospital by the weekend.

They were all very kind and gracious to him, but I saw some real frustration on their faces when they left the room. He was only 54 years old, too young to just give up and die, and they wanted him to keep on with treatments. He told one of them something that really touched my heart. He said, "Doc, the man you see here is not the man that I really am." Louie was a proud man, and he would rather not live, than to live in this state of complete dependence and helplessness.

In thinking back, I am not sure that I would not have done the same thing. He knew in his heart what I had sensed all along, that our lives would never be the same again. Not only was his body affected, but his thinking skills and vision were not the same. He had a great desire for life; I know of no one who enjoyed life any more than he, but his body was just not cooperating.

We did a lot of talking that day and the next. We discussed heaven and his funeral. We sang hymns together (as much as he was able), and we listened to some of his favorite gospel music. He was definitely ready to go. We cried together at the thought of having to be separated. He told me he did not want to leave, but he could not live this way, nor did he want me to do so either. He also said, in discussing heaven, "And just think, I won't have to get up any more!" Before the fall, it had become increasingly difficult for him to just get out of bed or a chair. He also spoke of wanting to see his dad.

Louie never did anything without thinking it through very carefully.

He always analyzed a problem from every angle. In his mind, this was the only solution, for all of us. If he could not be the man he used to be, and live his life in a productive way, he did not want to go on living. He did not realize, that the quality of his life had nothing to do with his abilities, which were numerous. The qualities that made him who he was, lay in his huge heart, his enjoyment of life, and in the way he gave so much of himself to others.

Outside of his room, the wheels were turning very slowly. As stated earlier, Louie was not ready for Hospice. The people involved in making the arrangements were deliberately delaying the plans to get him home to give him time to change his mind. This was a collaboration amongst our family, the doctors, and those responsible for making the arrangements.

In the meantime, I was being bombarded by family and friends, all of them telling me it was foolish for me to even consider taking him home. Everyone meant well, but they did not realize what it was doing to me, to have this constant barrage of people telling me what I needed to do. I was so burdened with all that was happening, I thought I was going to break under the pressure. But, God is faithful, and so is His Word. In the midst of all that was going on around me, a certain passage would suddenly spring up in my mind, and I would feel comforted again.

Louie's request to go home brought a large round of people that night and into the next day. His sons both came and listened as their dad tried to explain why he had made this decision. They spent the night again in the lounge. I just sat in the chair in the room and spent most of the night crying and praying. I found it so hard to believe, that the one who was chief at motivating others, had simply given up on himself!

On Thursday, Louie received a lengthy e-mail from Janet Dalton, encouraging him to keep on trying. She reminded him of some of his own words given to her during a time of difficulty for her. He said to her, "You keep your eyes on the goal; you lay aside all the negative things; and you never give up."

As for myself, I was just about out of 'wisdom' and motivation. I called Pastor Jim Harmeling the next morning. I guess he heard the desperation in my voice because he stated he was on the way down right then. Upon arriving, he spoke in a very forthright manner to Louie, saying that the goal Louie should have was to get back to school, whether on foot, or in a wheelchair, where his greatest sphere of influence was — with students. They talked quite a while; and when he left, Louie decided to stay at the hospital and begin the treatments again. I, along with family, and even his doctors and hospital staff, all breathed a sigh of relief.

I was so grateful to everyone who had a part in convincing him to keep going. Everywhere I turned, people were telling me I could not possibly take care of Louie at home. My mind told me this was true. Because of his physical size, his weakened condition, and his inability to walk, sit up alone, or even turn himself over in bed, it took three or four people to move him. As we had all tried to explain to him, Hospice would not be there every day, or at night. I knew I would not be able to go it alone at the house. He thought Josh or Justin could help. I explained they did not live with us, that we would need someone 24-hours a day.

The neurologist wanted to begin the treatment for the immune disease immediately, but the kidney doctors would not allow it until they had removed more of the fluid. They finally began treatment on July 6th. The treatments were a liter and a half of liquid per day, for five days. He took them two days; then they had to be stopped because of the condition of the kidneys. He was given more diuretics over the weekend.

By this time, I was certain, barring a miracle, Louie was not going home soon, nor in fact, ever leaving the hospital. Of course, I did not voice this to anyone, although I am quite sure there were many others who were thinking the same thing. There were just too many problems with his body; and there were too many things working against each other.

MONDAY, JULY 11, 2005

It was decided Louie could continue with the treatments for the immune disease. As one of his doctors said, "We can't just not do anything!" Louie took the treatments for three days. By Thursday night, he was showing signs of kidney failure and having difficulty breathing again. In fact, a code was called sometime during the night. I literally stood by his bedside all night. By the next night, I was so exhausted that I went to his mother's house to get some rest. Mike stayed with Louie. Needless to say, I did not get much sleep that night either, nor had I since all this had begun.

Early Saturday morning, I received an urgent call from Mike, stating a new doctor was on call and wanted Louie to undergo dialysis right away. Apparently, she had not read his chart. I dressed quickly and rushed back to the hospital, praying all the way. The storm was intensifying so much I did not know if I could withstand much more of it.

Mike and I talked extensively with the nurse. She said, that Louie, because of being somewhat disoriented that day, could not make the decision, and I would have to make it for him. My mind was reeling from all the information she had given us. I left the floor and went outside to sit down on a bench under a tree. Here I was, back in the same position I had been in 11 years earlier with Charles, having to make a decision that would determine whether my husband would live or die! I called Pam and told her the situation. She reminded me, "Mom, you don't have to make this decision. Louie has already made it. He has always said he would not have dialysis." How familiar those words sounded! They were almost identical to what I had told the doctor about Charles.

I went back upstairs and told the nurse we would not be doing the dialysis. As I think back, I know Louie was probably aware he would not live much longer. I am sure that was a factor in his decision not to have the dialysis. He probably wanted his last days to be spent in some measure of peace, not spent going through more procedures. The nurses wanted to start a morphine drip right away, but I asked if we could wait until Monday morning so we could have the remainder of the weekend together; although, I was not sure if he would make it that long.

Louie was withdrawn that day and spoke very little. Perhaps this happens when one knows his time is short. Perhaps this is an emotional withdrawal because it makes it easier to separate from our loved ones. At any rate, I knew I was not leaving the hospital until it was over. Mike left to go home.

Janet and Jennifer Lester, his two buddies of many years, appeared late in the evening on Saturday night. They had gotten word of what was taking place. Each of them spent individual time with him as I waited in the hallway. I could hear them laughing and joking together, just like old times. Later, as I walked down the hall with them as they were leaving, Jennifer said, "I just needed to be with the old Louie one more time." She also had come to try to convince him to take the dialysis and shared how her father had lived several years on dialysis. She naturally thought, if Louie took it, he could live longer also. But, Louie gently reminded her that her father was able to get up and move around, and he could not. Louie also told her, he knew he was going to die and stated he was okay with that.

Actually hearing him make that statement is the thing that got me through the next three days. Knowing he truly was ready was such a comfort to me as it had been with Charles. It gave me strength for what lay ahead for me. It is not just empty words when people try to comfort one another by saying, "Your loved one is in heaven and you will see them again." If you and your loved one have accepted Christ as your personal Savior, you know this is true, and these words do bring comfort to your spirit.

Someone once asked me how I had been able to handle all the hard things that had come into my life. My response was, that the little day-to-day aggravations bother me, but I seem to handle the major things at the time they are happening; then, I let go after it is all over. Louie once told me, I was able to handle difficulties because I was stoic, like my mother. The real truth is, that it is not I who is handling them; rather, it is God who is carrying me through those hard times.

After they left, I made my bed and lay down. And, the tears I had been holding back, began to fall. I thought Louie was sleeping. After a few minutes, he said, "P. J., are you okay?" "Oh yes, I'm fine," I answered. "That's good," he said, "I thought you were sick, and I was going to come over and take care of you."

This was the Louie I had always known. Even in his disoriented state, he was still trying to look after me. I reached over, patted his hand, and told him to go back to sleep. Before he did; however, I asked him one more time if he was sure about the dialysis. Again he said, "No." When I sat back down, I got out pen and paper and began planning his funeral.

Earlier, one of his doctors said he understood the decisions about the dialysis. Because of his condition and size, he realized I could not have cared for him at home. He would have had to be in a nursing home, and probably would not have made it long. I knew this, but having the decision confirmed, made it a lot easier to live with, even though it was basically Louie's call.

Louie coughed often that night. I knew the fluid was building up in his lungs. I could hear it in every cough. He also talked all night, closely akin to delirium. I finally asked a nurse, around 5:00 a.m. in the morning, if she could give him something that would help him sleep. Neither of us rested much that night.

On Sunday, the fluid was worse. He slept most of the day. Late in the afternoon, people began coming. Two of the principals and their wives came. Louie was more alert by this time and basically said his goodbyes to them. He had been especially close to these two men at the high school.

We were all standing in the hallway outside his room talking after Louie drifted off to sleep. A nurse went into the room to check on him. Suddenly, we heard Louie say, "Am I still here?" "Yes, Mr. Vesser, you are here at Ft. Sanders Hospital," she replied. Then Louie said, "Well, it sure takes a man a long time to die in this hospital!" We all burst into laughter. That was 'vintage' Louie! He, and I emphasize HE, had decided it was time for him to die, and he was impatient to get on with it! God is so gracious to grant us the ability to laugh at times like these. Even at some of his worst times, Louie could laugh and make jokes. He would not have been Louie had he not been able to do this.

Monday, July 18, 2005

It was a long, emotional night. Mike came and stayed part of the night. Neither of us slept. Louie woke up around 4:00 a.m. Monday morning. I was standing by his bed. I told him "Happy Anniversary!" It was July 18th, our seventh wedding anniversary. We began to talk, speaking of our love for each other, of our good marriage, and of all we had meant to each other. We reminisced about some of our favorite things we had done and all the fun we had experienced with our families. Over and over, we said, "I love you" to each other. I knew he was getting tired. I began singing some old hymns. He asked me to recite the 121st Psalm to him, as I had done once before. So, I did. It reads:

> 1 I lift up my eyes to the mountains—
> where does my help come from?
> 2 My help comes from the LORD,
> the Maker of heaven and earth.
>
> 3 He will not let your foot slip—
> He who watches over you will not slumber;
> 4 indeed, He who watches over Israel
> will neither slumber nor sleep.
>
> 5 The LORD watches over you—
> the LORD is your shade at your right hand;
> 6 the sun will not harm you by day,
> nor the moon by night.
>
> 7 The LORD will keep you from all harm—
> He will watch over your life;
> 8 the LORD will watch over your coming and going
> both now and forevermore. Psalm 121 (NIV)

I sang "Love Me Tender," all the while knowing, that my beloved was gradually slipping away from me.

Monday morning had come much too soon. I bathed early before the nursing shift changed. Louie kept talking about getting presents, that we had to have presents. I knew he was remembering somewhere in his mind, that it was our anniversary, and he thought he had to have presents for me. A nurse came and listened to his chest. She just shook her head and whispered that his lungs were full of fluid. They wanted to start the morphine drip right away, but I asked if they would wait until 8:00 a.m.

Doug had called the day before, wanting to visit, but I had discouraged him. I called him after the nurse left the room and said if he wanted to see Louie, he needed to come right away. He made it before 8:00 a.m. and got to say goodbye. He left at 8:30 a.m. and called Pam to get down there to be with me. She arrived around 9:30 a.m.. Shortly thereafter, Steven and Morgan, Sadie, Charlie, and Josh and Justin came in. We were all prepared to stay for however long Louie lingered with us.

I hope Louie felt the love in the room that day. I kept telling him how much I loved him. He responded in kind, at first, but as more morphine was administered, there was less and less response. We all just sat or stood in the room, or waited outside the door in the hallway.

We all thought he would have passed by afternoon, but that was not the case. I certainly did not want him to go, but I also did not want him to linger in his condition. I had been told that complete kidney failure was a painful death. But, I suppose the morphine was taking care of that. Later in the evening, I wondered out loud, how he could still be alive. Pam said, "I can tell you why he is still alive, Mom." "He's not going to die on your wedding anniversary!" There may have been some truth to that statement.

Some of Sadie's friends came by with food for us. I ate a little, but nothing had any real taste. I had not eaten all day, and I could tell my strength was going fast. Sometimes, I stood by the bed and held his hand. Sometimes, I laid my head on his pillow beside him. Finally, Steven brought a chair and placed it by the bed. He also brought a pillow and made me sit down. I never let go of Louie's hand, but I did doze off to sleep for a few minutes.

I was awakened by the sound of Pastor Jim's voice. I thought at first I was dreaming. Then, I realized he was actually there. He was telling Louie he was proud of him for continuing on and not giving up. It is said that hearing is the last thing that goes before death. I certainly hoped Louie heard the pastor's words.

As evening drew near, I had such a profound weariness, not just physical weariness, but a deep weariness of heart, soul, mind, and spirit. If you have been through the waiting with a loved one who is dying, you understand that of which I speak. It is a weariness that touches your very soul; and at the time, you wonder if it will ever go away. I also felt numb. I really had to remind myself that God's presence was in that room, not because I was feeling it, but because I claimed His promise that He would never leave me nor forsake me.

More people came; my sister, Shirley, and brother, Neill, their spouses, along with some of our friends, both from Morristown and Jefferson City. The nurses on the day shift came before they left, to tell me goodbye and to offer their prayers for our family. One of them told me they had discussed at the nurse's station, Louie's decision to decline the dialysis. They all agreed they did not know if they would have been courageous enough to do what he did. They did not know Louie Vesser! He was as strong and courageous in dying as he was in living.

Charlie took Louie's mother home later in the evening. She was worn out, and felt there was no reason for her to stay any longer. Louie had not been responsive all afternoon, nor had he opened his eyes. She had really said her goodbyes the day before, when he was more alert.

Louie's breathing became so labored! You could hear it out in the hallway. Sometime after midnight, I began softly singing the words to an old song, *Precious Lord, Take My Hand.* This song expresses what I am sure Louie would have stated, had he been able — that he was weak and weary, and that, as his life was nearing the end, he was asking God to take his hand, to walk with him, and to lead him home.

Pam was standing on the other side of the bed across from me, crying quietly as I sang. It was God who enabled me to sing. Once again, in His grace, He gave me what I needed for that particular time. I don't know if Louie heard me, but it was something I felt I had to do. It gave me comfort, as these lyrics reminded me, that God would lead Louie home.

Tuesday, July 19, 2005

It was around 12:30 a.m., when Janet appeared in the doorway of the room. She said she had just gone out to get groceries, and one hour later, she found herself getting off the 17th Street exit, heading for the hospital. It was strengthening to know she was there. I knew she was praying for us.

Justin, Morgan, Steven, and Charlie were all asleep around the room. Pam and I were standing by Louie's bed. It was now close to 1:00 a.m., Tuesday morning. His pulse was getting much weaker and his breathing even more labored. He would take a big breath and it would stop for what seemed like a long time. We would almost hold our breaths, thinking this was his last. Then, he would take another one. This happened several times. Mike came and stood with us.

I told Louie it was okay for him to go home to Jesus. The others joined me. That is all he had talked about the last couple of days, going home — not to Patriot Hills where we lived, but home, to Heaven. He often asked me, "P. J., when am I going home?" "I've got to go home." I would always answer, "Soon, Honey, it won't be long now."

The breathing got slower and slower. I knew the end was near. Pam woke up those who were sleeping, and we all gathered around his bed — Pam, Steven, Morgan, Justin, Charlie, Mike, and I. Janet had slipped in and was leaning against the wall at the foot of the bed. All of a sudden, God gave me a special gift. Louie opened his eyes briefly and looked at me — at least he seemed to be looking at me. I got to see his blue eyes one more time! I told him again I loved him and it was okay for him to go. I released him to the angels of heaven who had been present in that room, waiting to receive him and take him home. His last breath was little more than a sigh.

Immediately, from deep within me, welled up the song, *"The Doxology."* I had to sing because I knew praise was in order. By the time I was finished, everyone in that room was singing with me! We were not singing from our grief, but from joy that Louie's absence from us meant he was present with the Lord.

I walked over and hugged his son Justin and asked if he were okay.

He said he was, and then he gave me another gift, quite unexpected. He told me he had seen his Dad happier in the past seven years than he had ever seen him. Wow! That was really something special to hear! I went back over to the bed and leaned down and kissed Louie on the forehead one more time before the nurses were notified of his death.

Everyone began gathering their things and preparing to leave. Pam, Steven, and Morgan stayed to help me. There were 2½ months of 'stuff' in that room to be gathered up and taken home. The nurses came in and I signed papers. At one point, I said to Pam, "Where are my tears?" A few minutes later, it was as if someone had knocked my legs out from under me. I had to sit down and the tears came overflowing.

Someone once asked me if losing the second husband was any easier than losing the first one. Of course not! I had a unique love relationship with both men. The difference was, that Charles' heart attack and death were sudden and unexpected. I did not see it coming. Louie's illness was drawn out over 2½ months, and I knew ahead of time, he was going to die. The main difference is, that when you know in advance someone is going to die, you do a lot of your grieving in advance of the death. When it comes suddenly, of course, the grieving comes afterward. God was working; however, as I went into 'automatic pilot' again. Yet, for the second time in my life, I felt I had literally been split in two, and half of me was no longer there.

We thanked the nursing staff; some cried, and some hugged us. Then we started down to the elevators, leaving behind my Louie, after having spent 2½ months with him in that place. The realization was starting to sink in, that once again, my life was forever changed again and would never be the same.

Steven drove me home while Pam and Morgan followed in another car. Before we pulled out of the hospital driveway, Steven stopped and said a prayer for us. The ride home was quiet. There were many things going through my mind; however, like plans to be made, people to contact, and all the other things you have to do when there is a death.

We arrived at our home in Jefferson City around 4:00 a.m. in the morning, July 19th. We entered the house and put down our things. I had not been home in so long, the house seemed strange to me. We were all exhausted, and I was just about pushed to my limit, both physically and emotionally. I started toward our bedroom and came to a halt right in front of the door. I did not say a word, but I did not know if I could go into that room alone. Again, God provided for me, through Pam, who understood exactly what was going on in my heart. She came up behind me and said, "It's okay, Mom; I'm going to sleep with you tonight." Morgan came up behind Pam and said she was going to sleep with us too. The three of us piled on the bed together. It is a good thing I had a king-sized bed! As soon as we were getting settled, Steven came in with a pillow and blanket, and got into the recliner that was in the room — and we were, indeed, all together. That was another gift from my children — I did not have to sleep alone that first night at home.

People were at the house early the next morning, sharing our grief and offering their help. Jennifer Laster was there also and stayed most of the day. She made notes of everything I wanted done for Louie's funeral. She went back to the church and made all the arrangements for me. What a blessing she was! Later in the morning, we went to the funeral home to make arrangements there, and to take Louie's navy suit. We chose a beautiful, warm, wooden casket, and flowers in the Patriot colors of his school; red, white, and blue.

After lunch, the girls made me go to the bedroom to lie down. Of course, within five minutes, they were all on the bed with me, including three of the grandchildren! Robin Dawson came for a visit and walked into the room where we were. She just stopped and looked for a moment. "What a beautiful picture," she said, "of all your family gathered around you." And it was beautiful.

I do not know who was 'directing traffic' when people came to visit that day. It seems that everyone who came, ended up in the bedroom with us. We finally just got up and went into the kitchen and great room.

Danny Georges, our friend and staunch supporter through this whole ordeal, came in the afternoon to discuss his part in the service. I knew I wanted him to speak, because he had known Louie and me for many years, and he was the one who married us. Pastor Jim called, and I shared with him the one thing I wanted him to get across in his sermon; which was, that Louie did not give up, that he kept on trying to the end. I knew there would be many students present at the service who would need to hear that message. Louie was always encouraging students to do their best and keep striving for excellence in all they did.

On Wednesday morning, we went to the funeral home to view Louie's body. He had always opposed having an open casket, and I planned to honor that request at the church; but, I had to see for myself that everything was okay. Isn't it amazing how the lines of pain are erased in death! He looked so handsome, almost as if he were going to open his eyes any minute, and say something humorous. God's sustaining grace was upholding me at that casket. Our family stood together and talked, remembered, and laughed at some of his foolishness.

Upon returning home, I was looking through some papers that were on the desk there in the kitchen. I found a book of poetry from one of the writing classes at the high school. I thumbed through the book and came upon a poem that was put in by one of the students. I had never seen this book before and had no idea where it had been, nor why I had not seen it before Louie's fall. The title of the poem was *"When Tomorrow Starts Without Me."* I read it and the girls read it. We all cried when we finished it. It was as if Louie had left me a love letter from heaven.

The poem spoke of sadness at having to leave a loved one behind. It ended with these words:

> "So, when tomorrow starts without me,
> Do not think we are far apart,
> For every time you think of me,
> I am here — in your heart."
> ~Student Author Unknown

And that is where Louie will always be — in my heart. Thank you, Lord, for another generous covering of your Grace.

Wednesday, July 19, 2005

Wednesday morning came. I was remembering how Louie kept saying to me in the last two or three days, "Just your voice, P. J., just your voice." I did not know what he meant, and I never really had a chance to ask him. Perhaps he wanted only me in the room with him at the time; perhaps he wanted me to sing to him — I just did not know. On this particular day; however, I felt compelled to write down some of my thoughts about him. I went to the back porch where it was quiet and put on paper, my thoughts of him, and what he had meant to our family. Danny read this at the funeral that night; I entitled it, *"Ode to Pop."* I hope, Louie somehow heard my voice, coming through Danny's reading.

Amy and Mark came in sometime that day. They had been in Florida when Louie died. They had left the boys there, with their friends, and were going to fly back right after the funeral. I was glad I had all my family together to help me get through it.

The time for the receiving of friends was scheduled from 5:00 until 8:00 p.m., Wednesday night, July 20th, with the funeral beginning at 8:00 p.m. Jennifer suggested we should be there by 4:00 p.m., as there would be many people who would come. She was right! As we pulled into the parking lot, my heart started pounding in my chest. I felt such a heavy weight. It was déjà vu for me. It seemed only yesterday that I had walked exactly the same path on an evening in August; except it was 11 years ago, instead of yesterday.

As I entered the church foyer, people were already waiting to see us. I spoke briefly with each one and then entered the sanctuary. I was completely overwhelmed as I looked at the beautiful flowers, many in his school colors, flanking the casket. Jennifer had placed some pictures and his Assistant Principal of the Year award on stands around the casket. I just wanted to lay my head on that casket and weep until there were no more tears left. But, people were already coming down the aisle to greet us.

I took my place beside him and stood for the next four hours. Again, as was the case at Charles' funeral, I found myself comforting others, rather than being comforted. There was a steady stream of people, many of whom were students, expressing their own grief and needing a word of comfort. I tried to provide it as best I could. I leaned my elbow on the casket when I felt I could hold myself up no longer. I told one person that Louie had supported me all through our marriage and he was still holding me up.

We were all lined up in a single line out from the casket, all the people whom Louie loved the most — his family. That included his family and mine. This was the most somber time this group had ever spent together. Usually, there was teasing, laughter, and much foolishness, mostly due to Louie. Now, all we had were the memories of that laughter.

We went to the parlor before the service began. I asked Sadie if she would walk with me back into the service. Louie had told us in the ICU that we were the two women who had loved him the most in his life. It was important to me that I include her, and make her feel, as his mother, that she was just as important to this evening, as I was, as his wife. She took my arm, and we followed Pastor Jim and Danny into the sanctuary. The rest of the family followed close behind.

What a beautiful celebration of Louie's life! David Noonkesser, a longtime friend and colleague, spoke with humor, and of many funny stories of Louie's life. He also spoke of Louie's support and involvement in any type of program that benefitted students. He told of the positive and lasting effect Louie had on anyone who knew him. He ended with these words, "Louie Vesser, a job well done!"

As Dale walked up to the podium, I could sense his struggle. He and Louie had become very good friends in the short time they had worked together. He told a few more funny stories and spoke eloquently of Louie's love of life and influence for good on so many people. Then, he began singing; a cappella, the beautiful old song, "When They Ring Those Golden Bells." It was as though the gates of heaven had opened up! I think Louie would have loved having a song about bells sung at his funeral. I have rung handbells for many years and he had always called our group, "The Ding-A-Lings."

Danny was the next one to speak. He too, spoke of Louie's love of life and he used a quote that described him perfectly. It said, "I have come to live my life out loud." He mentioned Louie's taking me on so many

Saturday morning "adventures." He ended by saying, that on Tuesday morning, Louie had gone on the greatest adventure of his life when he entered the gates of heaven. Then, he read my comments, *"Ode to Pop."*

So many times, we pray for healing for a loved one, and it does not happen, at least not in this life. I realized with Charles, that my prayer had been answered, as he was healed in heaven. After Louie's death, someone told me, "God chose not to heal Louie, but to make him perfect." Thank you, Nancy Ann, for some Scriptural wisdom.

Then, Janet began singing the song *"Going Home."* Tears welled up in my eyes. I had known, early on, this song had to be used in his funeral, since going home was something he spoke of so often in his latter days. As the song ended, and Janet's voice was quietly fading away, I could almost picture Louie walking through the clouds and turning back to wave at us with that big, familiar grin on his face.

Pastor Jim came up to the podium. He spoke of all the things we leave behind; possessions, memories, etc., but that great men leave behind words and character. Louie's passing was marked by his words and character, and how he used them to positively impact the lives of others. He wanted to give up, but he did not. In the end, he put forth his best effort. He fought the good fight to the end. That is the legacy he left to his students and to our family.

After the message, Janet sang, *"I Bless Your Name."* As soon as I had heard this song the day before, I knew it was meant for Louie's service. It spoke of Paul and Silas in prison and how God opened their chains at midnight and released them. This was, for me, a picture of Louie's passing. The chains of a body, wracked by disease, were broken and he was released to go home to the Lord. Your love is abundant, Lord!

The last prayer was prayed and the final words were spoken. Everyone stood up. Sadie and I followed Louie on his last journey up the aisle of First Baptist Church. We stood in line for another hour or so in the church parlor to greet those who had not gotten to speak with us before the service. Then, we went home to prepare for the next hard day.

THURSDAY, JULY **20, 2005**

Thursday morning came early for us all. We moved about quietly, getting dressed, and preparing for the next difficult part of the week. Final goodbyes were going to be said to the one I had loved for 8½ years, to the one who had brought such joy and laughter back into my life after losing Charles.

We drove in Louie's Suburban so we could all ride together. As we moved down Highway 92, and passed the high school, an onslaught of tears came again. Louie had invested so much of his life and energies into that place and into the people there. Mark reached over and took my hand as he drove. To this day, I still have difficulty going to the school or even driving by it.

We drove to Lynnhurst Cemetery in Knoxville where Louie was to be buried beside his father. Originally, he had requested to be cremated. He did not know there was an extra lot in the Vesser family plot. Besides, I knew Sadie would not have been able to handle his being cremated; I am not sure I could have either. Yet, I understood why Louie had asked for cremation. He once said, he did not want to be buried beside Charles and me. I was so grateful to Sadie for providing this lot for his burial.

We arrived early, but there was already a long line of people there waiting to pay their respects to this remarkable man. Some had been at the funeral the night before, some had been unable to attend the funeral, still others were older friends of Sadie's who were unable to make the trip to Morristown the night before.

Thankfully, the service was short. Yet, it seemed this was all just a bad dream and I was going to wake up any minute and find Louie beside me. How could a casket hold the man who had been such an important part of my life?! How could I bear to never see him again, never hear his wonderful laugh, never feel his touch? And, I would never again hear him say, "P. J., you are an above-average bear!" I needed a huge dose of grace and God provided it. Pam was sitting beside me. I finally just lay my head on her shoulder and let the tears fall. I had tried to maintain some dignity, but it is hard to be dignified when your heart is breaking.

After the service was concluded, we spoke to more people, then drove to Sadie's house to have lunch and spend time together with both our families. I remember my son, Steven, telling Josh and Justin to try to keep in touch with me, as they were all I had left of Louie. After a short visit, we left and swung back by the cemetery and then went home. Mark and Amy had to fly back to Florida to retrieve the boys and drive their car back home. The rest of the family stayed on with me the rest of the week.

Exhaustion was an ever-present part of me. I had slept so little during my time at the hospital. One night, Pam ran a tub full of water and added bubble bath, lit some candles, and turned on some soft music. She said I was to cry, laugh, remember, or whatever I wanted to do, for as long as I wanted to do it. Then, she went out the door and closed it. I stayed in the tub for a long time; crying, thinking, remembering, and trying to sort out the events of the last 2½ months. I knew the real grief was still ahead of me as I began making my adjustments to life without Louie.

Part Three

The Days That Followed

In the days following the funeral, I went around in a daze, or so it seemed at the time. The season of grief, that had begun weeks earlier, continued to assault me. I once heard a pastor say, that you have to go through the valley of the shadow of death, to get to where victory awaits. I knew this was true from having lost Charles; but, when you are in that dark valley of grief, it is hard to see your way to the other side. Thank you, Lord, for your precious promises in the valleys and storms.

Yet, in the midst of grief, there were still decisions to be made, papers to be signed, bills to pay, and a hundred other details that required my attention. And there was always that constant ache in my heart that would not go away. In the dark of night, that ache became almost like a physical pain in my chest. Many times, I got up in the middle of the night when sleep eluded me. Thankfully, I was not fearful of being alone in my home at night; but, the loneliness was very real and always present. In those first days, there was no reprieve from the grief.

Steven was very helpful to me in handling some of the details. Mark also provided input and even came up one day to go with me to see my accountant. Both boys gave me wise counsel on financial matters and I was so grateful to both of them.

Pam was the one who knew the deepest feelings of my heart and shared the grief with me. One night, I was watching some home movies of our family. I became so overwrought that I called her to please come. She dropped everything, left her husband and two little girls at home, and came. We cried together and she held me. A person in grief, needs so much to be held! We watched more of the movies. I remember pointing out to her, that in every one of them, I was smiling or downright laughing. That was the life I lived with Louie, one filled with laughter.

Morgan also shared in my grief, as she loved Louie very much. Often, in church (I did not go back to choir for a long time), she would sit with me and just put her arm around me when emotion threatened to overwhelm me.

And what would I have done without my precious grandchildren? None of them were born when Charles died, so they were such a blessing during those hard days after Louie's death. This was another measure of God's wonderful grace.

Emily, Pam's oldest, who was three-years-old when Pop died, spoke of him often. She said he was in heaven and "Grandmom cries sometimes because she misses him." Once, she said, that when she goes to heaven, the first thing she is going to do is to give Pop a big hug.

When six-year-old Isabella, Steven's oldest child, had her dance recital that year, she asked her mom if there were video machines in heaven so someone could video her dancing and show it to Pop. He was the one who got her started in dance class when she was four. At Thanksgiving, six-year-old Tyler, Mark's oldest child, was given a paper to complete. The paper stated, "I am thankful for . . ." Tyler filled in the blank with the words, "My family and my Pop."

Louie had a special love and concern for each of the grandchildren. He once said we were going to spoil them, but not in the usual ways. We were going to take them to plays, fishing, ball games, etc., and introduce them to new and fun activities. We had done some things with Tyler and Isabella. He was already anticipating doing things with Emily and Shelton when they were four years of age; and later on, with Wil and Molly. I am so thankful they got to know their grandfather, especially when they did not know their first grandfather, Charles.

The holidays were so difficult! Thanksgiving was spent at Mark and Amy's house. The remarkable thing was, that not one person even mentioned Louie's name the whole day! I was struggling and they were all "walking on egg shells" around me. That is definitely not the thing to do! What I needed was to keep his memory alive by recalling funny things he had said or done. When he was not mentioned, it was as though he had never existed or been a part of our lives. I hope this was a learning experience for all of them.

One thing that was helpful to my recovery was making scrapbooks for Josh and Justin for Christmas that year. Louie had so many awards, all the way back to his college days, many of which, they were not aware. I gathered pictures and memorabilia from elementary school and on through college, as well as pictures of our two families. I felt it was so important for the boys to have a written record of all their dad's accomplishments, which were many. After Christmas, I began putting one together for me, one that was much more extensive, as I continued finding more papers. I am so glad to have this book to look back and remember.

Once again, I was thankful for my job as a preschool director and for the chance to be with young children. I was also thankful for my two teachers, Barbara and Vicki, who were with me when Charles died also. I needed a reason to get out of bed in the mornings. Yet, I have to admit, there were many days when I needed every bit of strength I could muster to do just that. Young children are so affectionate and I certainly needed their affection. This is one of the things you miss so much after the loss of a mate, just a hug, or someone to hold you in the middle of the night when you wake up frightened from a bad dream. Little children were able to supply at least a part of this need.

Friends, old and new, meant so much to me with their many acts of kindness. My yard was mowed for me for months; others cleaned out my landscaping, which had gotten really bad while I was spending so much time at the hospital; there were numerous dinner or lunch invitations; a teacher friend of Louie's helped me sell his Suburban; and the list goes on. The emotional support was phenomenal. Of special note; were the teachers and administrative staff at the high school; all the women in my Sunday School class; and Eleanor, Sandy, Mandy, Joyce, and Carolyn. My sister, Shirley, listened without hesitation any time I called needing to talk. God's grace and provision were in action through the actions of so many kind people. I claimed so many of His promises — no, I clung to them with a fervency like no other!

Billie, my friend and Louie's, and her son Josh, were so thoughtful. They brought me flowers often because it was something they knew Louie did often. Danny Georges always hugged me every time he saw me in church and so did Pastor Jim. He also visited me several times in my home in those earlier days, and just sat and listened. Janet and Jennifer were available when I needed to reminisce and tell "Louie stories." When we would get together, we might start out crying, but we always ended up laughing!

And then there was Sadie, Louie's mother, my rock, the one to whom I really poured out my heart. She was not just my mother-in-law, but she became one of my best friends. I think we both needed each other so much in those difficult days. I could talk about Louie all I wanted, and she never minded. I think the same was true for her. I will never forget her faithfulness during the hospital stay. She was constantly doing things for me, from washing my clothes, to sitting with Louie so I could get out for a time, to slipping me some money to help with my expenses. She is a woman who gives much to anyone who has a need and I am so grateful to have her love and friendship.

I am also grateful I did not have to deal with *Made In Tennessee*, the business Louie had started many years ago. In the latter two years of his life, he knew his health was fading, and he began trying to sell the business. It did not sell right away, so he ended up selling the building. We brought the business to our basement and continued operation from there. He really wanted to keep this business to have something to do when he retired from education. Yet, after bringing it to our home, he seemed to lose all interest in it. I was the one who handled the operation from then on. In January of 2005, he began trying to sell the entire business. In May, four days before he fell and broke his hip, his sister-in-law, Cheryl, and we, signed the papers for the sale of *Made In Tennessee*. Talk about timing! Who, but God, could have ordained this happening at that particular time! His timing is never too soon or too late, but always right on time, regardless of how much we fret.

In August, Pam Morgan and Amy, rented a lovely cabin for us in the mountains of Gatlinburg for three days. We took Emily and Isabella with us. It was so good to get away, but also heartbreaking at times. There were places we went that brought to mind other times spent there with Louie. We had always enjoyed the mountains so much. The girls and I did have some times of laughter among the tears.

I believe each of us grieves in different ways. When my father died, my mother could not wait to get his things out of the closet. When Charles died, she told me to get his things out of the house as quickly as possible. But, I could not bear to part with them yet. Having them hanging there in our shared closet made it seem as if he were still there. It was many months before I could do anything with them.

Louie and I had separate closets. Again, as with Charles, I could not bring myself to part with his clothes. His boys had taken some of his things, but the rest hung there for a year or longer. I used to go into the closet and bury my face in one of his suits, trying to recall the scent of him. Eventually, I gave them away to a man who had MS and had gained a lot of weight. I knew Louie would have been pleased with my decision.

It is very hard to cook for one person. I found myself doing a lot of snacking instead of eating properly, or going out to eat (with anyone who asked me!). It was a long time before I could bring myself to sit down at our kitchen table alone. Most of the time, I would carry my food on a tray to the recliner and eat there in front of the television.

TRIBUTES TO LOUIE

The following, are accounts of the numerous tributes given to Louie that year. The first was, the *"Night of the Patriots."* It was held in November in honor of our war veterans. It also highlighted the talents of the many students that were involved. This is a program of which Louie was in charge at JCHS and was one of the largest and best attended events of the whole school year.

That year's program was entitled, *"Larger Than Life."* Of course, it was a tribute to Louie. His picture was in the background on the front page of the printed program. A presentation was made to me by Dale Schneitman, who was the principal and Louie's friend. It was two scrapbooks filled to overflowing with notes and letters from faculty and students, each of them sharing what Louie had meant to them and the school. They also highlighted a large, framed picture of him, while a young student sang the Barbara Streisand song, *"Memories."* All of Louie's family and friends, and many of the faculty and others who were attendance, were in tears when the song ended. When I got home, I stayed up until midnight reading what everyone had to say. It is always comforting to hear good things being said about a loved one who has passed away.

The next big event was the Jefferson County Chamber of Commerce Banquet in January, 2006. Louie had been gone six months. He was posthumously awarded the *"Jefferson Countian of the Year"* award, one of the most prestigious awards given in the county. Five hundred people gave a standing ovation when his name was called as the recipient. I made my way up to the platform to receive the award for him. I had prayed for a week that I would be able to accept it without being emotional. And I was able to do just that! When I returned to my seat, Mandy whispered that I had done it with such grace. I quickly whispered back and assured her it was not by my grace, but God's grace, that had enabled me. Steven was my 'date' for the evening. When he arrived to pick me up at the house, he had brought me flowers and was very sweet and attentive. It seems Isabella had told him to bring flowers because "it's what Pop would do."

On the way out, I stopped to get my coat and make a donation to the Leadership Class, another of the programs started by Louie. Their project was the coat-check; thus, the donation. I told them what a good job they were doing, and they actually applauded me! I still could see God's handiwork of grace at work.

Another big event was held in April, the FCA (Fellowship of Christian Athletes) brunch called, "Bloom." Louie had started this event the year before, as a fundraiser for the FCA, to send some of the students to camp. The FCA program had just about died at the school, and he had revived it to the point that it was going strong again. This event was also held as a memorial to Louie. Sadie and Morgan attended with me. Of course, we were all three emotional through most of it. A beautiful tribute was paid to Louie by one of the mothers who had worked with him on the original brunch. At the end of her talk, some of the FCA girls did an interpretive dance to a song by Chris Rice, which speaks of ". . . flying to Jesus." I know Louie would have been somewhat embarrassed at all the attention being paid to him; but, it was a balm to my spirit to know that others recognized what a remarkable man he was and just how much he contributed in his short lifetime.

There had been other times and events in previous years, when I felt he should have received more recognition than was given to him. Those were the times when he always said, "P. J., it's not about me; it's about the kids." That was his philosophy of life, doing what would benefit others, without thought of taking credit for himself.

There were many other tributes, including a letter from Michael R. Williams, Speaker Pro Tempore, and a proclamation from the Senate of the State of Tennessee. The proclamation honored his memory and his "commitment to living the examined life with courage and conviction." He received a similar proclamation when he was awarded the Vice Principal of the Year Award for the State of Tennessee.

But, the last really significant tribute was the graduation ceremony held in May. Dale spoke with emotion of Louie and his tremendous contributions to the high school. Then, he awarded a young woman, the first *"Louie Vesser Memorial Scholarship"* award, to a student who had worked closely with Louie on so many projects. I was proud to have been a small part of the committee and the selection of the first recipient. Also, the recipient of the *"Jefferson Countian of the Year"* award always received a large grandfather clock. This year, I had asked that the money for the purchase of the clock be given to this scholarship fund. I believe he would have been very pleased at this gesture.

THE JOURNEY OUT

I both anticipated and dreaded being out of school for the summer. I was really tired when it was over, so for the first few days, I pretty much did nothing. Summer was our time together when we would go on those 'adventures' that he loved so much. Some days I just wandered around the house; crying, and asking God what I was supposed to be doing. I felt so lost.

It was around this time, I learned Steven and Morgan were expecting another baby. "The Lord gives and the Lord takes away." It was going to be good having another little one around to help ease the pain of being without Louie.

In July, Pam, and the girls and I, went to the beach in Savannah. She had told me, back in March, she was going to get me out of town on the anniversary of Louie's death. Doug had to be in China that week, so we loaded the car on July 15th and headed out. It was a quiet week. Pam missed Doug, and there were times when I could not hide the sadness I felt. On the day of the anniversary, we were all down at the beach. I took a long walk and did of a lot of thinking and 'talking' to Louie. I came to the realization that I could not continue living in the past and that I needed to get on with my life. I even felt a peace about selling the house and moving back to Morristown, something I had been thinking about for some time. I really needed to be with my family.

I believed this was what Louie would have wanted for me. He once told me he did not worry about me, as far as the future was concerned, because he knew my children would always be there to take care of me. This was spoken long before his illness. One has to wonder if people are sometimes allowed some foreknowledge of the future. At any rate, I could hear in my head Louie saying, "P. J., it's time to get on with it!"

Although I did have peace about selling the house, I knew it would still be difficult to leave it. The day I married Louie, I went to the house in Morristown, where Charles and I had lived for 20 years of our married life. I walked through every room and remembered. When I left the house and locked the door, I did not look back. I knew I was moving to Jefferson

City and starting a new life. This time; however, when I moved back to Morristown, I was going alone, which meant, I was moving from one empty house to another. My heart was still in the house we had built and loved, but I also realized, a house is just bricks and mortar, and not Louie. He was in my heart, and would be with me, regardless of where I lived.

In late August, after I had started back to work, Steven gave me some other news that rocked my world again. He had been offered a wonderful new job opportunity with his company. The only problem was that it meant a move somewhere up north. I was so proud of him, but I felt such a great sense of loss. I know I was spoiled by having my children so close by; but, I was beginning to feel that God was slowly taking away all those people I loved, and on whom I depended so much. Still, even though I acknowledged that my dependence should be on God, and Him alone, as I had gotten older and was alone, it was a matter of concern to me. I had to remind myself again, of the numerous promises from God's Word of His continued presence in my life.

I found myself getting busier and busier in 2006. There were days when I left the house at 7:00 a.m. in the morning and did not return until dinnertime or later. Just anything to keep from being in that empty house! All the television, books, or music did not change that. It was really difficult to go from a very active and fulfilling lifestyle to one that was so much quieter.

I tried to fill my life with family, job, and church activities. My grandchildren, and the children at the preschool, did much to help heal my hurts; but, even my own children did not understand the deep sense of loss that I felt, nor the loneliness. No one can really understand unless one has experienced the same type of loss.

I got more involved in the Music Ministry again. We had a new Minister of Music, and I began directing the four- and five-year-old children's choir again. This was a tremendous blessing to me. In October, I sang a solo for the first time since Louie's death. I sang *"His Eye Is On The Sparrow,"* which was somewhat of a testimony of God's care for me. It was also a favorite of my friend, Peggy Bible, who had passed away in June. She was the one who had gotten me started working with children, originally, and had been one of my chief supporters when I started the preschool at our church. As I began to sing, I said a silent, "This is for you, Peggy!"

I also sang in the Living Christmas Tree again. I did not sing the first Christmas after Louie died. As I participated in the rehearsals, and climbing up to my spot in the tree, I realized one day, that my joy in life was slowly returning and some of the terrible weight of sadness I had been carrying for so long, was being lifted from my heart and spirit. I was able to genuinely laugh again! This happened after Charles' death too, but not until I met Louie. This time; however, as I contemplated what was taking place in my heart, I realized it was not because of another man in my life, but simply because God was filling my heart with His joy!

To add to my joy, about two weeks before Christmas, I had a dream one night about Louie. I had always wondered why a mate, with whom we share our deepest thoughts and feelings, could die, go to heaven, and never have another thought of the one they have left behind. In the dream, I was sitting at some type of information desk and looked up to see a man standing in the outer hallway. I thought he looked like Louie. I turned back momentarily to the desk, then looked up again. Louie was standing right in front of me. He was wearing his gray suit, and of all things, was sporting a mustache! Under his arm, he carried the notebook he always carried to school. There was instant recognition for both of us, but no acknowledgment of that recognition. He asked if I lived around there. I told him no. He paused for a moment, then asked if I were okay, with an intense look on his face. I said, "Yes." Another pause, then he smiled ever so slightly, nodded his head, and walked away. It was as if I had been given some assurance that I had not been forgotten and that he still had concern for my welfare. I sensed it through this bizarre dream. Is this Scriptural? Probably not. But it sure gave me some comfort.

Time passes and life goes on, whether you wish it to, or not. Hours passed into days, days into weeks, and weeks into months. Once again, as in 1994, my life was changed dramatically, both inwardly and outwardly. Loneliness overwhelmed me at times. Once, someone told me I was not alone. No, I was not alone, but I was very lonely. There is a difference. Although my married friends were kind to include me in some of their outings, I was still somewhat uncomfortable, being a single person in a world where, at least in my world, everything seemed geared to married couples. After you have been married for so many of your adult years, it is difficult to suddenly wear a new label — 'single.'

It is as though you have to redefine who you are, both mentally and emotionally. I will say, that my friends, Dale and Eleanor, are one couple with whom I did not feel like the proverbial 'fifth wheel,' as I did with some others. This is probably because our friendship went back for so many years.

I certainly was not ready, after only seven years of marriage, for it to end so abruptly. There were so many facets to our relationship; that Louie's passing, left a tremendous void in my heart. For whatever reason, this was what God had ordained for my life at that time and I had to accept what He had chosen for me. I knew God was working to 'mend' me again, just as He did after Charles' death.

Little Emily, who was four at the time, and I, had several discussions about heaven and her Pop. Once, she asked what people do in heaven and what was Pop doing. I told her there was a lot of beautiful music, with everyone praising God, and that everyone was happy and healthy. That seemed to satisfy her.

Right after he died, Amy shared a thought she had about Louie. She said, "I like to think, when Louie got to heaven, Charles went up to him, shook his hand, and said, "Thank you for taking care of Peggy." I also had a picture in my mind as well. I pictured Louie and Charles sitting together under a tree by the river. Louie was telling him all about our wonderful grandchildren, none of whom Charles got to see. Of course, all of this is just speculation. But, somehow, these pictures brought me a measure of comfort.

My second Christmas without Louie came and went. It was much the same as it had always been in our family, except for the absence of much of the fun and laughter he seemed to bring to our celebrations. When it was over, and all the packages were opened and put away, and everyone had gone back to their own homes, I found myself on my knees beside my bed, much the same as I had done in January of 1997. Again, I prayed that God would teach me to be content with my life, and to show me how to be of service to others.

New Year's Eve, 2006 had come. A year and a half had passed so very quickly! I was sitting in my home awaiting the new year, contemplating what changes, if any, might be in store for me.

Sometime after Charles died, I had a sense of anticipation about my future. Of course, I had no idea what was ahead, and certainly was not thinking of a new husband in my future! I hoped that I could have that same sense of anticipation again. Or perhaps, my life was just to be lived, day-by-day, fully trusting God, and whatever was in store for me.

WHAT I LEARNED | A TESTAMENT

I am thankful for many things. I am thankful that I was given another chance at happiness, albeit short. I am thankful that I was loved by such a man as Louie Vesser, from whom, I learned so much. I am thankful God sustained me during those hospital days and afterward, that He brought me through yet another very large storm — and He walked with me through it all. I am thankful for the many promises He gave me, assuring me of His continued presence, for His provision for my needs, and for the grace that continues to sustain me daily.

Louie was a large man in stature. Janet once told me I had looked beyond his size and saw his heart. One could not be around him very long without seeing the size of his heart and the special gifts he possessed. Pastor Jim asked him once, what his goal was in life. His reply was, that he wanted to make a difference in the lives of people and be a positive influence. I believe he accomplished this, as evidenced by so many people who attended his funeral, and by the hundreds of notes, cards, and letters we received during his illness and death.

In remembering Louie, and our life together, I think of great love, much laughter, wisdom, sensitivity to my needs, and a genuine concern for my well-being. I remember once I had an appointment in Morristown. I was very nauseous the whole time I was there. I received a call from him while I was there and told him how I was feeling. When I left to go to my car, he was sitting outside waiting for me. He had driven all the way up from Jefferson City to bring me a Sprite. He followed me closely all the way home. This is just one example of the kind of caring I received from him all our married life.

One of his greatest gifts to me, that probably aided in my recovery, was his helping me to become more independent, and by encouraging me, that I could be, or do, anything I wished to do. That is a rare gift to leave a mate; but then, Louie was a rare and special man.

In thinking back over my life, I realize that the whole of my life has been a testament to God's grace. Through His grace, God granted me the love of not one, but two fine Christian men, each one remarkable and exceptional in his own way. How blessed I have been! There are many women who have not had the blessing of one good man, much less two! And, who but God, could have granted me the grace that enabled me to say goodbye to these same two men as they made their journey to heaven.

Through both of these experiences, I have learned that grief is a process made up of different stages, a journey where sometimes the road is smooth, but oftentimes, it is very rough, filled with ruts and boulders. Healing does not always come quickly, it takes time and determination to 'keep on keeping on.'

Grief is an emotional wound that requires the right kind of care for healing to take place. And just as physical wounds can leave scars, so can emotional wounds leave unseen scars. Perhaps, the emotional scars are left on our hearts to remind us of how God has worked in our lives, and how He has redeemed us from the hold grief can have on our lives.

Once again, as with Charles' death, God proved Himself faithful, over and over again, in countless ways. Through these two major storms in my life, I came to know Him in ways I might not have otherwise known Him. He has been my Comforter, my Provider, my Protector, and my Friend, the One in whom I could confide when there was no other, the Uplifter of my head when my joy was almost gone, the One who took away my fears.

Of course, there were times of questioning. That is our human side. That is where living by faith comes in. And I am sure there are answers I will never have in this life. When I get to heaven, and stand in the presence of my Savior, the questions will no longer matter anyway. I also have accepted that death and change are a part of life and how I respond to them is entirely up to me.

Yes, I was broken by grief, not once, but twice. But each time, I was also restored by an abundance of God's grace being showered upon me. For that, I am eternally grateful. I find, that I no longer have to ask the question, "Where are you, Lord?" He is right where He has always been throughout my trials — living in my heart, loving me, comforting me, providing for me, sustaining me, calming my fears, and keeping me safe beneath His wings. This is where I want to be, always, and into eternity.

"Sing unto the Lord a new song;". . . so says, Psalm 96:1 (NIV)

I pray, that in my remaining years, I will be singing a new song, one that is always filled with praise and thanksgiving, even though there may be more songs laced with sorrow and pain. If, and when, things come my way that I don't know how to handle, or if another storm comes through my life, I can look back and remember these past storms, and be confident of His presence and His peace, knowing, that if He brought me through all of this, He is certainly able to handle anything else that may come my way.

> "For the Lord is good and His love endures forever; His faithfulness continues through all generations."
>
> Psalm 100:5 (NIV)

Epilogue

As of this writing, it is now January, 2017. Charles has been gone for 22 years, and Louie, for 11 years. Perhaps, the reader wonders where I am at this stage of my life.

In 2006, after the first anniversary of Louie's death, I began feeling that I should move back to Morristown, where I was born and lived all my life until Louie and I were married. My reasons were; that part of my family was still there; my job at First Baptist Church was there (a 35-mile round trip every day); it was also the church I attended regularly, and was involved in many of its ministries, and my friends of many years were still there. But perhaps, the greatest reason was, that the house in which I was living, where there had been so much love and laughter, was now empty of both.

I sold the house in 2007, without a realtor — yes, I, who had very little knowledge of such matters. For this reason, and in every decision I had to make (and there were many!), I knew God's hand was guiding me. Otherwise, I could not have pulled it off! I purchased a smaller house in Morristown, near my daughter, Pam, and am still living in it today.

However, it is never the same when you go 'back home.' I now live in a different part of town, with different neighbors, who have become new friends. But, my old friends are still the same. In fact, we just seemed to 'pick up where we left off.' As time has passed, I have adapted to the changes and it feels like 'home' again.

In May, 2015, I retired from my job of 33 years, as the director of Weekday Early Education (WEE School), a preschool program of our church. It was a difficult decision, as I have always enjoyed working with young children. Once again, I began getting the feeling that it was time for a change in my life, that I needed to step aside from this position. I was reminded of a passage of Scripture that seemed to bring this decision home to me, one that meant something to me after Charles died; it was Isaiah 43: 18-19:

"Forget the former things, do not dwell on the past. See, I am doing a new thing! . . ."

It also goes on to say that,
". . . I am making a way in the wilderness . . ." (NIV)

Wow! That last phrase really spoke to me! I am not a very spontaneous person; I like to plan ahead, and know what is ahead. Through this passage, I have confidence that God will make a roadway for me and will be with me wherever that road may lead.

Our Ten Beautiful Grandchildren

Nowadays, I live a fairly simple life, one of contentment. I enjoy spending time with my family. There are 10 grandchildren now. They bring me joy when we are all together; there is always something going on, and much fun and laughter. I am also learning to do some new things since my retirement, such as learning to play the piano, a dream I have always had. I am also considering some new ministry opportunities.

On New Year's Day this year, I was visiting with my son, Steven, and his family. We were all sitting down to brunch when my daughter-in-law, Morgan, asked that each one share what he/she would like to be doing this same time next year. I sat thinking and listening to the teenagers, and their humorous comments flying around the table. Then I said, "First of all, I just want to <u>be</u> here this time next year! I want to enjoy the new year, spending time with family and friends, and I would like to do some good along the way." Perhaps that is the purpose of this book — to provide some good to someone who might read it.

Dear Reader, if you are a Christian, and you are going through a storm or trial, my desire is that this book will bring you encouragement and hope. If you are not a Christian, and you also are going through a difficult time in your life, I hope the reading of my story will cause you to want to seek the God of whom I have written. He loves you so much that He sent His Son to die for you; and He desires to have a relationship with you, and be your Lord and Savior.

I am already praying for each one who reads this book, that God will use my experience to meet a need in your life, whether it be for comfort and healing, or for finding the One who gives us not only comfort and healing, but eternal peace.

May God Bless each of you,
Peggy Skaggs Vesser

If you have enjoyed this book,
or if it has helped you in some way,
we would love to hear from you.

PLEASE CONTACT US AT:

Peggy Skaggs Vesser
EMAIL: PSV2017BROKENNESS@GMAIL.COM
ADDRESS: PO Box 1164, TALBOTT, TN 37877-1164

Printed in the United States
By Bookmasters